The Chosen Journey of Life

Volume I of III

A Look at Relationships

SIR JUSTUS ABRAMELECH

The Chosen Journey Of Life
Copyright © 2024 by Sir Justus Abramelech

ISBN
978-1-957378-42-8 (Paperback)
978-1-957378-41-1 (eBook)

Table of Contents

Foreword by Sir Justus Abramelech

Even if dysfunction is more prevalent than ever in many houses, our good must step up to protect honor.

We must be accountable for doing what is right in order to administer justice in the family.

I am grateful for Yahushua's enlightenment, who is the Most High of all the Earth and Heavens. Since we were created in the likeness of our Creator, we have a duty to use our gifts to further the purposes of our Father.

If you can see dysfunction and assist someone in overcoming it, you will be rewarded.

In order to inherit immortality and more on earth, one must revere thy parents and authorities in their lives.

Hello, It is I!

After more than 400 years, the moment has arrived for people from all nations and regions of the world to break free from their chains of servitude.

The United States of America: the land of the Free or the Oppressed?

I was born in Newark, New Jersey, during the 20th century's black power struggle and civil rights era as the oldest of four siblings. Growing up in Irvington, a diverse urban neighborhood outside of Newark, there was peace and happiness in our neighborhoods. Newark marked the start of years spent on this Native American soil, now known as the United States, before the Brick City projects were demolished. My identity and power started to develop in the middle of the 1970s. I would sow seeds and make things out of my imagination, learning the basics of life. Even though I didn't know about universal rules when I started my study in Irvington in the early 1980s, I stayed true to myself because I wanted to know who was actually valuable. Small gangs started to form in my neighborhood in the later 1980s. A carefree neighborhood where I could play football, ride bikes down the street, or even just hang out in the park with my pals Corey, Sir, and Marcus was ruined by the generation of teenagers who were five to seven years older. I learned not to trust everyone when unnecessary roughness and dishonesty entered the situation.

Lenny, who was in a higher grade than me, was a child of an Italian family who lived across the street. Lenny's father was a businessman who worked for himself, and he had two or three older sisters. He was a cool dude. We played football while making fun of one another. Hakeem, his mother, and his sister Safiya lived next door. Hakeem was comparable in age to my brother. Hakeem liked tricks and raced very quickly. Back then, I didn't have the life experience to identify warning signs of death or bid my friends goodbye.

I wasn't sure whether I would ever see the unspoken words again, but they gave me a glimpse of an untold memory. My parents abruptly departed our neighborhood in 1989 without saying goodbye. As I moved south, I pondered what had become of them. I was given the option of staying with my mother in the south until the house was sold or traveling to New Jersey with my father (with a cold turkey sandwich as an inducement). There was a lot on the line, but because I understand how love works, I decided to leave what was meant to be left behind.

I wasn't sure whether I would ever see the unspoken words again, but they gave me a glimpse of an untold memory. My parents abruptly departed our neighborhood in 1989 without saying goodbye to treasured connections. As I moved south, I pondered what had become of them. I was given the option of staying with my mother in the south until the house was sold or traveling to New Jersey with my father (with a cold turkey sandwich as an inducement). There was a lot on the line, but because I understood how love works, I decided to leave what was meant to be left behind.

Later in life, I understood that having a happy family depends on having strong interpersonal bonds with friends and family. I had a good childhood compared to other kids. Despite their difficulties, my parents always tried to keep the family together.

However, there were instances when I felt tense with my mother because she talked over me and I was unable to properly express myself. I felt it to be a very unsettling situation. I simply stopped paying attention to the chat whenever I thought the results of her "musings" would make me feel less confident.

I frequently kept my opinions to myself in order to avoid criticism. I made the decision to follow the easiest route in order to avoid bad circumstances. When verbal communication felt emotionally overwhelming as a child, I learned to tune it out. It made me insensitive to a woman's worries and feelings. How was I supposed to defend myself to her or any other emotional woman? My father never taught me how to be patient when speaking to women. But dad also taught me to respect others, not to shake hands with everyone, to speak in a polite manner to strangers, and to observe in order to pick up new skills. He taught me to wait patiently for what I want and to live by the faith of my job. Whenever my biological father visited or took us out, he was generous with spending. A noticeable entourage of well-wishers accompanied him wherever he went, creating a vivid memory of him moving about. Despite his reluctance to engage in arguments or be swayed from his decisions, he never wavered in expressing his love for my mother.

While my stepfather might not have offered extensive emotional support, he compensated with an incredible work ethic. Despite the sacrifice of spending time away from his family, he tirelessly worked. He possessed a profound love for the Word of God and thoroughly enjoyed engaging in conversations with people. His knack for managing others allowed him to de-escalate situations smoothly, standing firm on his convictions without causing offense. He shared his life experiences with those who made time for him, but when work called, he knew when to let go and focus on the task at hand.

Regardless of the incident in the past where my mother judged me, I picked up the habit only to discover that as long as I bring harm to others, my heart would never be clean. Despite the imperfections I could see, she taught me a lot of principles that much exceeded them. She gave me the ability to be creative. To help you with your work, you must find resources. She fostered a strong work ethic that included being meticulous and tidy, rising early, and getting enough rest. Performing research to discover the truth, making snap decisions, speaking up for justice, and speaking out against injustice, in addition to acting quickly to achieve objectives. She has shown me how to develop family values that will foster harmony and aid those in need. I will always respect and love my parents, and I am very grateful to them.

Ridicule can lower your self-esteem. This will remain even when one grows up. Therefore, I abandoned the concept of condemning one's past to validate my argument, realizing that love can never come this way. True love is the work of forgiveness, it has no accusations or remembrance of the past to force an argument.

Consequently, I have gained a low tolerance in dealing with perpetual emotional situations that hold my past against me. Nor do I want to not acknowledge the wrong or ignorant circumstance. Can this be true love? To talk over someone else in order to express one's thoughts while ignoring the other person? Once more, I would leave a persistently emotional circumstance in order to find serenity. I detest being inactive and will take all appropriate measures to be fruitful in order for life to proliferate abundantly.

In 1989, the golden age of hip-hop brought about the sanity and happiness of adapting to a rural way of living. The humid and muggy heat would make the day all about sleeping with the AC on or it would be too miserable and exhausting to walk. I remained indoors mostly to tinker with computers and video games rather than complain about boredom. In Hawkinsville, Georgia, there existed a separate educational system for children in elementary, middle, and high school.

The seventh grade of middle school awaited my arrival in 1989. I was academically well ahead of my contemporaries, and since I wasn't challenged, until the conclusion of high school, no real attempt was made to excel. My peers put me to the test to determine my strength, mentality, and associational capability. However, because of who I am and how I do not regard prejudice, stereotypes, or other extremes, I was able to observe the strength, mindset, and competence of my companions because they were afraid to act in the same way as me for fear of being reprimanded. I had realized that the teachers of the other race had used a variety of tactics to instill fear in my comrades in order to control their behavior and attitude.

Besides the (adjective) tone of voice used to emphasize a point, partiality towards others, expulsion from school trips, and etc. I witnessed all of which was new to me, it was evident that some teachers used fear as a weapon of intimidation amongst those who identity was different.

My recap on entering Hawkinsville High school from middle school felt like a system devised for the division of labor. Seventy percent of the students placed in general education was of native descent. Many of their parents who lacked education beyond high school felt inferior to speak up for what was best for their children. Was this school-based curriculum devised to keep the majority learning on an inferior level? Giving options from a school counselor to opt out of College Prep and Vocational for General. Again, the connections I made in seventh grade were lost as I enrolled for College Prep.

Under six of the seventy percent of students enrolled in college prep were of Native descent. Higher learning was offered to the minority of us among those born into education.

My recollection of high school can attest that many of us remained in trouble, whether it was intentional or not. My friend Warren called me "Too Cool" for my actions expressed liberty as I was not bothered by the things most of us were. Often times, I rarely recalled occasions of other races in the principals' office as I once was and so many of us were sent for disciplinary action. Over the course of high school, my peers excelled mostly in the discipline of sports rather than academics. Mr. Hailey, the man of the hour, taught me the fundamental laws of electronics, a passion of mine since a youth. Because of his excitement, I was intrigued to learning more each day. I realized my talent for history came naturally to my recollection as the conception of stories read from the scholarly words of my German teacher. Mrs. Zell taught European and American history without the violent atrocities that gave rise to power. Decent were my high school teachers, however both of Hailey and Zell were exceptional in the ability to lay down a good foundation joyfully to advance my learning.

Hawkinsville high school's mascot, a Red Devil, was the emblem on the trophy given in recognition to students who excelled in sports and academia. One day, my youngest brother brought home a trophy. After some time, my mother grew weary of the tension within our home and had recognized that something had to be done about the trophy's presence in our home. The trophy had become an idol of confusion that had broken our peace. A realization of consequences for bringing idols into our home was explained to us as my brother reached for a hammer and smashed it to pieces. "Despite the past I hold no grudges as I understand the circumstance. I cannot forget my friend Ashley who saved my life at Crystal Lake. I have always known to recognize the hearts of good people who care. Peace be unto him."

I cherished wonderful moments growing up alongside my brothers and sisters. We had a blast playing Foursquare and exchanging music, with my brothers showcasing their impressive ability to recall numbers from memory. Our backyard was the arena for epic 3-pointer contests, and we spent countless hours immersed in the world of Nintendo and Sega Genesis games.

MTV raps and BET was my center of music in the 1990's for the local radio stations gave no ear play for hip-hop. Near the end of graduation, the majority of students removed their caps, but I kept mine on. I was relieved to have completed my time in Hawkinsville and was eager to begin anew in our company. From previous conversations, my mother was aware of my desire to become an electronic engineer and the need that any institution I attended for further education had to be run by Native Americans. I entered Tuskegee University (TU), the college of my choice, as a young man without having received any advice from my father about how to treat women with respect or how to take education seriously. After, three years had passed, a tragic moment in life occurred that I regained myself and acquire a new skill. I sought manual labor and realized this is not the life for me as I applied for an opportunity in sales.

My mother was an incredible parent, ensuring we had all our needs met, especially concerning food and a life free from troubled environments. She shielded us from adults who posed harm to children and actively supported other parents in advocating for their children's rights. Emphasizing the importance of faith, she made sure we regularly attended church and studied the Word of God, laying a strong moral foundation rooted in truth and accountability.

Her approach to life was interpersonal, teaching us the values of fairness and trustworthiness through actions that aligned with what is right. She treated everyone with decency, never showing favoritism or partiality. Despite our unique relationships with her, she treated each of us with the fairness and respect that continues to this day. Now, as I reflect on her sacrifices, it's my duty to honor and repay her for a lifetime dedicated to our happiness.

My mother exemplified the essence of family unity and moral integrity by ensuring that we were not isolated from my father's side of the family. She went beyond her relations and included everyone, bridging differences that arose from her connection with my biological father.

Consequently, after two years in Sales, I knew it was time to further my education to achieve what I had longed for. I enrolled at Middle Georgia Technical College (MGTC) in the Electronics Communications Program. I turned down a six-month electronics internship offer from the Warner Robins Air Force Base since I had no intention of staying in that part of middle Georgia for very long. In order to transfer to DeVry University, I enrolled in a second program and was the first to graduate with a degree in electronics computer technology.

I wanted to go to DeVry University for my engineering degree because I intended to relocate to Atlanta in 2000. I had the good fortune to be able to transfer credits from my two associate degrees and certifications from MGTC and TU. After graduating with a degree in Electronic Engineering two years later, I chose to pursue a second bachelor's degree in computer engineering the following year because I was dissatisfied with the state of the economy. I entered Keller University's Master of Business Administration degree right away. I wanted to be able to raise my children without having to worry about education getting in the way. After being in the program for a few months, I understood that I needed a master's degree in project management and information systems in order to be happy. I had a contractual job in the cable and hosting sectors. I finished three master's degrees three years later and was prepared to start a new family.

I got married near the conclusion of my second master's program and moved into a new house when my first son was born. I had no experience or knowledge of how to ask her father for permission to take over control of her under my leadership in order to start a new family. She gave birth to my second son, who is three years and two months older than my daughter, the youngest of the three, 18 months later.

After the cable industry, I got expertise in a number of sectors, including the IT technology, health care, and package delivery & shipping solutions. In the latter sector, I established my professional designation as a Sr. Data Analyst.

As a young man, I underestimated the importance of life's true value while searching for the right companionship to share spiritual insights and pursue my life's purpose. Unfortunately, a lack of involvement and understanding led to growing distances among my brothers and sisters. However, as I mature, I've come to realize the significance of maintaining strong connections with family. It has become clear that nurturing these relationships is essential as I strive for the quality of life I envision. Collaborating with them not only contributes to my well-being but also empowers us all to make choices that lead to a collectively happy and fulfilling future. Together, we can trust in the support of one another and share in the blessings of success, reaching the pinnacle summit of joy.

After ten years of marriage, new challenges emerged that drove me to the brink of insanity, forcing me to reevaluate reality and redefine who I am in the service of family governance. I don't consider myself to be conservative, and I don't rely on anyone to run my life. Any method created to manage family business revokes the ability to develop for the divine purpose for which one was made.

My life experiences have led me to evaluate morals, laws, and marriage in particular as well as other relationships and ideals. To make sure the commitment of loving kindness is always present, I have grown more aware of our behavior both within and outside the home. The guy who upholds the seat of power in honor of his home is comparable to an honorable judge who, in addition to making provisions (through business), also looks out for his family out of compassion and love in order to govern justly. One pursues money through the business as a way of life.

Can a covenant be made without a guy present if his home serves as his courtroom? Let every man be intelligent to impart authoritative guidance to live modestly protecting the hearts to provide the safety of love that conveys tranquility in harmony. I have a lot of nice things to say about women, especially those who are noble in their consideration of people from other backgrounds and cultures while displaying no hostility and possessing a fierce desire to fight for love. These women are a tremendous help to a meek man who prefers to live in harmony and avoid quarreling over trivial matters. I must admit that the woman is the rightful owner of the home since she creates space for expanding the business and transforming the house into a welcoming haven of love where everyone may find rest and happiness. As the owner of the house and the children with her husband, a woman is more valuable than anything else and is much wanted. She encourages and teaches her girls and sons to be independent.

Greater than the man who is of the world, there is a life force outside of the sphere of man. Who has the right to grant authority to all men? Can a man defy the nature he was born with? All life depends on a natural habitat that offers shelter and food in exchange for job satisfaction. However, the frustration of desolation inflicted upon others to take what has not been gained honestly suffers the wicked. They eventually circle back to the beginning to contemplate their actions or perish in the dusk invited.

I proclaim all these words to you that you may know that I have nothing to hide. There is no choice for me to be ignorant of what I do or what others have done. Especially, if brought to the attention of one and it remains hidden from the truth. What qualities of witness bring about peace so that everyone might be free? The decision to hide the truth is no longer made out of ignorance, but rather out of a lack of empathy, which fuels the motivation behind atrocities committed. For as long as I am alive, I aim to be unrestricted in my pursuit of a faithful freewill lifestyle that the Universe will bless according to goodwill of humanity so that I may bless others with my presence of goodness.

Who Am I intro

Who am I that shall write all that matters on a sheet of paper to the intent of some edification that the weak may be esteemed?

My testimony lives by the spirit of grace, mercy, and truth for a greater witness of things not seen yet believed.

Who am I that I may find a companion to utter my thoughts as one would a confidant?

My strength is made perfect in weakness to know the ways of the meek.

Who I am is a man seeking the honor of a few, a righteous remnant held to the utmost regard for his Father's word of instruction and reproof to do that which is right in his omniscience.

I perceive light in my father's eyes.

Who I am, a man redeemed by a price of honor that the sacrifice of life has been laid down for friends and those lost might be saved. Let my time be mine only, but for the works of my Father's glorious kingdom be revealed. I live by compassion, mercy, and truth which by nature is full of grace for promise of life and peace throughout my days seeking justice to do judgment. Help me to find that good thing that pleases you O' ABBA throughout my days that I bring forth the substance of righteousness as it pertains to saints to enter the eternal covenant of life.

Justice served without excuse for Israel's sake have Yahu'shua suffered. His name is One, the Most High God of Abraham, Isaac, and Jacob took our infirmities, wounded for our transgressions, bruised for our iniquities, and bare our sicknesses for righteousness' sake. Count it all joy that we approach the hour of darkness, enduring with love to overcome trials of tribulation, making our calling and election sure to be redeemed at that day when wickedness is no more. What a mighty great cloud of witness this shall be to see the anointed rejoice "Glory to the Creator of the Heavens and Earth" Hallelujah!

Question Yourself to Know Your Purpose

Is it ok if questions challenge you and are you willing to find the answers to what you don't know?

A citizen cannot sit a bench, everyone was born with purpose! What is your name and why was it given?

Do you know the full meaning, origin, and proper pronunciation?

Were you not called by name from the womb? How shall you then meet your Maker?

What is the purpose of your journey?

What is your status of where you are in your journey? What does your life mean?

Why are you here?

Who are you and are you on the right path? How do you know your destiny?

Are you predestined to find the higher power of goodwill? Does your spirit align in truth with your heart?

How far do you seek to know questions not understood by most?

What honor do you have for the essence of your spirit? Has nature revealed universal laws to you?

Can you integrate change in your way of life from that which you came?

Which haplo-group is your most current common ancestor found?

Do you know who you are now and your purpose?

A citizen cannot sit a bench, while humanity is at stake!

Embrace the Peace

The state of restlessness is disturbed by the stillness at the center of love. To glimpse the reflected nature of your inner self is to experience calm in its purest form. Where internal conflict exists, the tension's driving force is truth's mirroring nature, which replenishes youth. We cherish peace because it brings us joy when our hearts are pure. Be careful not to pull the card from under pressure but rather to release it gradually as you express it verbally, slowly, and emotionally. Guard peace with all your heart, might, and soul knowing that your being is the expression of light that penetrates the soul of all mortals as we jump over hurdles. Join forces to create and savor the tranquility of this existence we regard as good. We appreciate your explanation of how to embrace peace.

Principles of Life

The keys of humanity are in the hearts of all who apply the fundamental principles of life daily. Humanity is like bringing heaven on earth that the ethics for living establish peace throughout the land. Heaven is like a paradise for all to dwell safely having an absence of evil; all mankind upholds a noble honor to love one another as himself.

The fundamental principles of life consist of living in harmony in respect for all relationships. All who focuses on the development of character for the sake of integrity to maintain honor, peace, humility, patience, and long-suffering as a necessity for dignity; shall receive mercy and compassionate love as one's lifestyle becomes a royal code of ethics noteworthy of godliness.

The nobles of the land are all who contend for peace. Generally, the nobles of such merit hold an office in the title of a prince or priest. A prince or priest is accredited with the loyalty of good faith and valor to govern oneself uprightly and the wellbeing of others to carry out selfless acts of service.

The office of a Prince is one that matures over time. The quality of a young princes' heart may be very pure in nature; however, the experience of life's circumstances has not given him the depth of wisdom needed to fully execute decisions in a sound manner. An office of a young prince is implied as room for growth for the potential errors in judgment that may occur; as his heart is still learning to search out matters in its capacity before giving an account of partial knowledge. Overtime, a young prince is able to build a strong kingdom fortifying it through continuous acts of good service.

Whether the young prince is found unreliable; his office would be noted as weak. Eventually, his office including all relationships are considered of none effect. On the contrary, a prince who designates an office of reliable service is blameless. A prince having a primary focus of resilience to endure over time establishes excellence in relationships for the extension of his office. The office of a priest is like unto a prince or king for the manner of mercy and peace reigning in one's heart so that an unbiased judgment proceeds from an understanding heart and divine wisdom.

A priest or prince having a good conscience warrants one to be a defender of an upright faith, morally sound and most honorable in the sight of all divine and majestic powers of authority. The continuous conscious act to defend such faith gives license to a royal office abiding in justice. The ability to serve in this capacity is thankworthy as one dwells in an imperfect society making a difference resolves conflicts and dissolve the burdens of many. In any imperfect society there will be difficult times where royal counsel becomes a necessity to handle many relationships so that none are tarnished. As the relationship matures a prince or priest may intercede for needs of circumstance to console the affliction.

The noble defenders of the faith who uphold peace in the land for all mankind are revered as honorable. The prince or priest is known to apply the fundamental principles of life throughout their relationships in a royal manner that brings heaven on earth. Their office is to serve mankind with an upright heart that instills peace and safety for all to dwell in a land undefiled.

As a young prince matures in service it is his duty and conscious effort to become faithful in executing decisions soundly to develop his office of maintaining relationships for excellence. A wise prince or priest generally plans royal counsel for the provision of handling diverse affairs.

Just as he prince or priest are the noble defenders of the universe; the princess or ambassador are also a force to be reckoned as masters of a united front. The office of a princess is guided by her wisdom of things not ruled by fortune. The fortune of a princess is solely based upon her love for her people. Therefore, her fortune lies within her people, who cheerfully give gifts for the work she has performed. A princess does not use masculine energy to rule over people as her influence is solely based upon the commitment to serve others in the accountability of their acknowledgement.

A princess extends her hand to those in need of substance without overexertion of herself; allowing a nourishment that is reciprocal of what goes out to come back. A princess's heart is filled with compassion to search out matters of equity, justice, and loyalty. Outside her realm, she discovers things that make life rewarding as it fulfills her thirst in doing good for others. A princess not only welcomes, but is welcomed and blessed by those within her presence.

A princess is a diamond in a ruff, a beauty impenetrable to look upon. Good intentions without defeat is the sobriety of others to perform an office beyond those of society. Her diplomacy is to awaken the flaws that stop the conscience from the concerns of her royal advisors, counselors, and the best of friends adhere to a high moral code of ethics in regard of humanity. The benefit of society is her pleasure. Seeking counsel always before an unknown matter is carefully approached to be more familiar of a situation than not to be. Like unto the ambassador, the patience of timing is always considered as the dealings of others present. Provisions are made for those in need to assist in the wellbeing of life surrounded by her.

The royal ambassador is the hand of welcome representing the honor of authority granted. Intelligence and the wisdom of relationships is her security that overcome obstacles that obstruct peace. An ambassador is the representation of the highest honor bestowed upon her province in foreign lands. Seeking the pursuit of common relations, the ambassador is a great communicator, making the complex simple for the sake of strength in unity. Never at the mercy of time, is she patient for things to take place in its proper time. Knowing that the good shall overcome the situations at hand. The ambassador is always pleasant in appearance, ready to serve and put in motion the things that seemed impossible on the behalf of the people to be respected by all.

The ambassador's entrance is the most radiant color of beauty that fills the heart with peace as joy is the expression of it. Understanding legacy, history is no mystery to matters abroad. Having a commonwealth in the establishment of a people economically and socially are people at home to be entreated of all issues that makes abiding in the universal laws of life wonderful. Her ethics are among the highest, having paradise in mind of those impoverished. Her craftsmanship is the great relations of kingdoms, businesses, and provinces, the handling of any diplomatic issue is performed honorably.

Signs of Respect

What might be a nice sign of respect if you're a gentleman, you can do a slight nod… and some women, if they feel pleased, to do a little bob.

A princess should wait for one to extend their hand if they do, then she must remember not to be excited and shake too hard, be nice and gentle.

Gift giving is also part of the etiquette when meeting royalty, royal etiquette dress code is generally conservative though it is acceptable for women to sport little sleeveless dresses.

Self-confidence, knowledge of Self

Many of us think we know ourselves thoroughly, I realize how much I don't know myself when I am caught buying something that is not me, investing time and money that I'm not good at, forcing myself to do something I really don't want to do.

Other ways that 'one does not know herself exhibits this by putting up airs, doing something only because she thinks it will make her look rich, elegant, and sophisticated, she tries too hard to impress, she does something only for her image.

A root meaning of the word, "elegant" is authenticity, which is one of the keys to self-confidence, to know yourself makes you become secure within yourself.

Many women have secret struggles with self-confidence and self-esteem, there are many roots of this issue to discuss.

Gaining elegant self-confidence has a lot to do with authenticity, it's a matter of discovering who you are, what our heavenly father has given you in talents, aptitudes and aspirations, dreams, and what is in your hand.

How does one be authentic?

Start by taking an inventory of yourself

I. Take some time to discover your likes and dislikes.

II. What are your strengths, talents, and dreams? YAH put them there for a reason.

III. What do you think about all the time? It is your passion.

IV. What is in your hand? What can you do? Assess the opportunities around you.

The Life of a Prince
or Princess

A Princess is Magnified by her Glory of Love

The Attributes of a Princess

1. A princess generally wears dresses; her apparel is arrayed to beautify her countenance while providing comfort and elegance.

2. A princess always keeps her head covering bright for happiness, straightforwardness, and glowing with a beauty having no shame.

3. A princess is always polite and considerate of others' feelings; she is not contentious nor conspires against authority for gain.

4. A princess sees everything as beautiful and exciting; she creates from her passion the imagination to fulfill her vision.

5. A princess always shares with those less fortunate; her hand and heart never suffer others to experience loss without care.

6. A princess is always learning new things: especially from her elders, she learns from the mistakes of others and patiently takes time to understand a matter.

7. A princess always tries to do her best at any school of thought, she applies all that is learned and reserves what is not applicable.

8. A princess is confident, but not a snob, she is not conceited in her own interests: but of others of importance.

9. A princess believes in herself and believes that dreams can come true, she is secure in her life being truthful without partiality.

10. A princess's heart is of mirth, she holds no resentment that becomes bitterness of heart even stubbornness whose end is rebellion.

The Prince is Magnified by his Honor of Love

The Attributes of a Prince

1. A prince has several important teachers that would guide his training in learning the manners and customs of being a royal person. Usually, belts were also worn at the hips to provide support to the trousers.

2. A prince is educated in various martial arts, travel, and outdoor activities such as horse riding, hunting, and others.

3. A prince would also need to take a keen interest in the management of the estate he would inherit and defense of his estate, the well-being of tenants, food, water, and sanitation would be important issues. He works to increase value in people and in situations.

4. Piety is an important part of the life of a prince and princess to never forget the poor.

5. Humanity, focuses on good, never harm. Inspires confidence in and from others.

6. Royalty, always cares for the family with loving, respectful interactions. Each person is loved, valued, and nurtured. Builds respectfully with all people as they interact in their community – including the global community. Family members know they are special and live in a royal household:

7. A prince trains to live an honorable life in YAH'S kingdom and is a major asset of the royal family according to his relationships.

8. A prince invests and re-invests, starting with people that are closest – and then circling outward.

9. A prince's management of life resources is considered with eagerness to meet basic needs. Provides the best quality budget allows – never overspending, squandering, or over-indulging.

10. A prince works with energy, purpose, and a plan (no laziness). Invests available time in purposeful activities. Time is the measure of work for the outcome of success. Repetition is the mother's milk of success. Lastly, finding deals and budgeting work, puts in a full, quality day.

Freedom Of Abundance

Unlocking your heart and mind to overcome fear, stagnation, even procrastination to live the lifestyle you desire is a transformative journey that involves personal growth, self-discovery, and mental empowerment. Here's an overview of steps to help you avoid falling victim to a game of emotions headed on the wrong path:

1. Self-Awareness: Begin by understanding yourself, your fears, and the reasons for your stagnation. Reflect on your beliefs, values, and past experiences that may have contributed to these feelings.

2. Set Clear Goals: Define what the lifestyle you desire looks like. Set specific, achievable goals that align with your vision. Having clear objectives provides direction and motivation.

3. Challenge Your Beliefs: Examine your limiting beliefs and negative thought patterns. Identify the stories you tell yourself that hold you back. Challenge these beliefs and replace them with empowering, positive ones.

4. Mindfulness and Meditation: Practice mindfulness and meditation to quiet the mind, reduce anxiety, and increase self-awareness. These techniques can help you manage fear and stay present.

5. Educate Yourself: Knowledge is empowering. Learn about the areas of life related to your desired lifestyle. Seek out books, courses, mentors, and other resources that can guide you.

6. Action and Consistency: Overcoming fear and stagnation often requires action. Take small, manageable steps toward your goals and maintain consistency. Progress, no matter how small, is encouraging.

7. Positive Visualization: Use the power of positive visualization. Imagine yourself living the lifestyle you desire in vivid detail. This can boost your confidence and motivation.

8. Affirmations: Employ positive affirmations to rewire your subconscious mind. Regularly repeat affirmations that reinforce your abilities, worthiness, and potential for success.

9. Surround Yourself with Support: Connect with a support system. Share your goals and fears with trusted friends or a mentor who can provide guidance, encouragement, and accountability.

10. Embrace Failure: Understand that failure is a natural part of growth. Rather than fearing it, view it as an opportunity to learn and improve.

11. Gratitude Practice: Cultivate gratitude for what you have and for the steps you've taken. A grateful mindset can shift your focus from scarcity to abundance.

12. Take Care of Your Health: Physical health and mental well-being are closely linked. Prioritize exercise, a balanced diet, and adequate sleep to ensure your body and mind are in optimal condition.

13. Adaptability: Be open to adjusting your plans as needed. Life is full of surprises, and the ability to adapt to change is a valuable skill on your journey.

14. Patience: Transforming your life and overcoming fear takes time. Be patient with yourself and acknowledge the progress you make, no matter how slow it may seem.

15. Celebrate Successes: Celebrate your achievements, no matter how small. Acknowledging your successes boosts your confidence and motivation.

Remember that unlocking your heart and mind to achieve the lifestyle you desire is a continuous process. It's about personal growth, self-improvement, and aligning your actions with your vision. Embrace the journey, and don't let fear or stagnation hold you back from living the life you truly want.

If you're ready to unlock genuine emotional and mental freedom in your financial life, the time has come to tap into boundless wealth. When your core beliefs don't align with the abundance you desire and deserve, the Emotional Freedom Technique (EFT) can help you release the thoughts, emotions, and convictions that obstruct your path to manifesting the financial prosperity you seek.

Emotional Freedom Technique (Self-Development)

The Emotional Freedom Technique (EFT), often referred to as "tapping," is a psychological acupressure technique used to alleviate emotional distress, reduce stress, and manage various psychological and physical issues. Developed in the 1990s by Gary Craig, EFT is based on the principles of traditional Chinese medicine and combines cognitive therapy with acupressure.

Here's an explanation and the processes involved to accomplish Emotional Freedom Technique:

1. Understanding EFT:

    EFT is based on the belief that emotional and psychological issues are caused by disruptions in the body's energy system. These disruptions can be thought of as energy blockages or imbalances.

2. The EFT Process:

    Setup: The process begins with a "setup statement" in which the individual acknowledges the issue they want to address. This statement usually begins with "Even though I have [problem], I deeply and completely accept myself."

    Tapping Points: EFT involves tapping specific points on the body while repeating affirmations related to the issue being addressed. The primary tapping points include the top of the head, eyebrows, side of the eye, under the eye, under the nose, under the mouth, collarbone, under the arm, and the karate chop point on the side of the hand.

3. Addressing Specific Issues:

    EFT can be used to address a wide range of issues, including stress, anxiety, phobias, trauma, pain management, weight loss, and more. Each session is customized to the individual's specific concern.

4. The Tapping Process:

    During the tapping process, the individual acknowledges their issue and any associated negative emotions or feelings. While focusing on the problem, they tap on the specific acupressure points.

5. Affirmations and Validation:

    EFT often combines the tapping process with positive affirmations that help reframe negative beliefs or thoughts. The goal is to shift from a negative emotional state to a more positive and accepting one.

6. The SUDS Scale:

    EFT frequently uses a Subjective Units of Distress (SUDS) scale to measure the intensity of a negative emotion or issue before and after the tapping session. The individual rates their distress level on a scale of 0 to 10, with 10 being the most distressing.

7. Repetition:

    The EFT process is often repeated several times in a single session until the individual experiences a significant reduction in emotional distress or reaches a state of emotional relief.

8. Self-Help and Professional Guidance:

   EFT can be practiced as a self-help technique, and many resources and guides are available to help individuals use it on their own. However, some people seek the guidance of trained EFT practitioners or therapists for more complex or deeply rooted issues.

9. Research and Effectiveness:

   EFT has gained attention from the scientific community and has been the subject of research in psychology and holistic health. Some studies suggest that EFT can be effective in reducing symptoms of anxiety, phobias, and post-traumatic stress disorder (PTSD), but more research is needed to establish its long-term effectiveness.

10. Safety and Caution:

    EFT is generally considered safe and non-invasive. However, individuals with serious psychological conditions should seek professional guidance and should not rely solely on EFT as a treatment method.

    EFT is a versatile and holistic approach to emotional and psychological well-being. Many people find it to be a useful tool for managing stress, addressing emotional issues, and promoting a sense of emotional freedom and well-being.

Universal Laws (Self-Mastery)

The Universal Laws, often referred to as the "laws of life" or "laws of the universe," are a set of principles or rules that are believed to govern the way the world works. When understood and applied effectively, these laws can indeed be seen as a roadmap to having whatever you desire in life. Let's explore how the Universal Laws can be considered the rules to the game of life:

1. Law of Attraction: This is perhaps the most well-known of the Universal Laws. It suggests that like attracts like, meaning that the energy and thoughts you emit into the universe will attract similar energy and experiences. When played right, understanding and using the Law of Attraction can help you manifest your desires. By maintaining a positive mindset and focusing on what you want, you can draw those experiences and opportunities into your life.

2. Law of Cause and Effect (Karma): This law teaches us that every action has consequences. If you want positive outcomes, you need to engage in positive actions. By understanding the Law of Cause and Effect, you can consciously make choices that lead to the results you desire.

3. Law of Vibration: This law explains that everything has a vibrational frequency. Your thoughts and emotions also carry vibrations. When you raise your personal vibration by cultivating positive thoughts and emotions, you become a magnet for similar high-vibration experiences and people.

4. Law of Correspondence: As above, so below. This law suggests that there is a correspondence between the macrocosm (the universe) and the microcosm (individuals). By understanding this law, you can learn to see how your inner world (thoughts, emotions, beliefs) is mirrored in your external reality. This insight allows you to change your inner world to influence your external experiences.

5. Law of Balance (Yin and Yang): This law highlights the importance of balance. Life is a dynamic interplay of opposites - light and dark, good and bad, joy and sorrow. Recognizing the need for balance in your life helps you make choices that lead to equilibrium, enhancing your overall well-being.

6. Law of Inspired Action: While your thoughts and intentions are crucial, action is also necessary. This law teaches that inspired, purposeful action is required to bring your desires to fruition. By taking action that aligns with your intentions, you actively participate in creating the life you want.

7. Law of Divine Oneness: This law underscores the interconnectedness of all living beings and the universe. When you recognize that we are all part of a larger whole, you can approach life with empathy, understanding, and a desire to contribute positively to the greater collective. This, in turn, can lead to a richer and more fulfilling life.

In summary, the Universal Laws can indeed be seen as the "rules" to the game of life. When you understand these principles and apply them effectively, you have the potential to create the life you desire. However, it's important to remember that playing the game of life skillfully requires continuous learning, self-awareness, and conscious choices. While the Universal Laws provide a framework, it's up to each individual to engage with them and use them to their advantage. Here are the rules of the game for reflection of your daily life:

THE LAW OF CORRESPONDENCE (MIRRORS):

Everything you perceive in your external reality is a reflection of your inner world. As within, so without. You are intimately connected to the entire universe. When faced with challenging situations or people, ask yourself, "What within me attracted this experience, and what can I learn from it?" The power to change your reality lies within you.

THE LAW OF CAUSE & EFFECT (KARMA):

The energy you put out into the world returns to you. Your actions have consequences, and what you sow is what you reap. By making choices aligned with the reality you desire, you can shape your world.

THE LAW OF ATTRACTION (MAGNETISM):

You possess the innate ability to attract what you desire. Let go of what no longer serves you, as it can hinder your magnetic power. By understanding your worth and embracing your authentic self, you amplify your ability to attract your desires.

THE LAW OF COMPENSATION:

Your financial rewards are a reflection of your personal growth and the positive impact you make in the world. Giving and receiving are interconnected; to receive, you must open yourself to it.

THE LAW OF RECIPROCITY (AYNI):

Giving without expecting in return multiplies your blessings. The true source of abundance is not people but the universe. What you give with an open heart returns to you through diverse channels.

THE LAW OF TRANSMUTATION:

With focused intention, you can transform any energy into what you desire. Your authentic self and purposeful life can inspire others to follow their own paths. Energy is constantly shifting and transforming.

THE LAW OF PURPOSE (DHARMA):

Your purpose is less about what you do and more about who you are being. By expressing your authentic self, you naturally gravitate towards your unique talents and gifts, fulfilling your purpose.

THE LAW OF POLARITY (CONTRAST):

Contrast provides clarity and helps you define what you truly want. Embrace adversity and challenges as opportunities for growth. The meaning you assign to situations is key to your perspective.

THE LAW OF VIBRATION (CONTINUOUS MOTION):

Change is constant, and you can choose to either resist it or flow with it. Your thoughts, feelings, and energy vibrations influence your reality. You are a unique point of consciousness, and your frequency shapes your experiences.

THE LAW OF PATTERNS (RHYTHM):

Patterns reflect internal conflicts or alignment. Ignoring patterns allows them to become more pervasive. Recognize the lessons within patterns to shift your energy and vibrations.

THE LAW OF BALANCE (YING YANG):

Manifestation is a balance of action and surrender. Both are required for success. Knowing when to act and when to let go prevents burnout and attachment.

THE LAW OF RELATIVITY:

Challenges and experiences do not define your worth. They are opportunities to learn and grow. Perspective is everything, and gratitude provides valuable context.

THE LAW OF INSPIRED ACTION:

Achieving your desires requires both mental alignment and action. Inspired action is guided by intuition, belief, and the understanding that you are always supported.

The Law of Divine Oneness (INFINITE POSSIBILITIES):

Miracles exist, and there are infinite possibilities in the universe. Embrace the belief that "anything is possible," aligning you with this limitless law.

THE LAW OF FREE WILL:

Your choices, decisions, and actions are your own to make. You have the power to create and shape your reality. Your free will is governed by intention, unwavering faith, and the determination to pursue your deepest desires.

Embrace them. Contemplate them. Delve into their depths. Meditate on these timeless principles for a win-win game of life outcome. They will unfailingly reappear as recurring themes throughout your life's journey. Notice their presence in your life and your interactions with each law. Are you fully harnessing the potential of each law in your daily life? Revisit this resource periodically to explore how your comprehension of these laws and your engagement with them transform over time. Always remember to do your affirmations/exercises morning and evening: Consciousness is of paramount importance.

Access Your Subconscious Mind with Binaural Beats:

Binaural Beats work by delivering one distinct frequency to your left ear and a subtly adjusted frequency to your right ear. This ingenious setup prompts your brain to effortlessly generate a third frequency, an entirely internal creation. This third frequency serves as a powerful tool to induce altered states of consciousness, aiding you in achieving relaxation, heightened focus, improved sleep, and more.

Incorporating the theta frequency is designed to assist in reducing your brainwaves, making it easier to access your subconscious mind.

Play to Win (Freedom Abundance Game)

Live life to the fullest for an abundance of heart and mind with No Fear. The relationship between Emotional Freedom Technique (EFT) and the Universal Laws lies in their shared focus on the power of consciousness and the influence of one's thoughts and emotions on one's life experiences. Both EFT and the Universal Laws can be seen as complementary tools for personal growth and well-being.

1. Law of Attraction: EFT and the Law of Attraction are closely related. The Law of Attraction posits that like attracts like, and your thoughts and emotions influence what you attract into your life. EFT, by addressing and releasing negative emotions and beliefs, can help align your thoughts and emotions with your desired outcomes, making you a more effective practitioner of the Law of Attraction.

2. Law of Cause and Effect (Karma): EFT recognizes that emotional issues and beliefs can be the cause of various emotional and physical effects in your life. By using EFT to resolve these issues, you can change the causes and, therefore, alter the effects you experience.

3. Law of Vibration: EFT acknowledges that emotions have their own vibrational frequencies, and by tapping and addressing these emotions, you are effectively working with the Law of Vibration. As you release negative emotions, you raise your vibrational frequency, which can attract more positive experiences.

4. Law of Correspondence: EFT encourages introspection by asking individuals to explore the root causes of their emotional issues. This is in line with the Law of Correspondence, which

suggests that what you see in your external reality is often a reflection of your internal state.

5. Law of Balance (Yin and Yang): EFT seeks to balance emotional and energetic disturbances by tapping on acupressure points, which can be viewed as an application of the Law of Balance. It aims to harmonize the flow of energy within the body.

6. Law of Inspired Action: EFT is an action-oriented technique that involves tapping on specific points while addressing emotional issues. This aligns with the Law of Inspired Action, which emphasizes the importance of taking action to manifest your desires.

7. Law of Divine Oneness: The Law of Divine Oneness asserts that we are all interconnected and that there is a universal consciousness. EFT practitioners often emphasize the interconnectedness of emotions, beliefs, and physical well-being, reflecting an understanding of the oneness of all aspects of life.

The connection between EFT and the Universal Laws is that they both acknowledge the significance of the mind, emotions, and consciousness in shaping one's reality. EFT can be seen as a practical technique to work with these universal principles, helping individuals to release emotional blocks, align their thoughts and emotions with their desires, and ultimately create a more harmonious and fulfilling life in accordance with these universal laws.

Be Fruitful and Multiply

Having knowledge of the creation pertaining to the gift of life is inherent for the earth to bless you abiding in the principles of life that gives reign to the dominion entrusted as a good steward of faith. Through good deeds of morality and experience in one's craft or skill, life can be navigated through the palm of the hand. The palm of your hand gives you access to things within reach, these are the connections you beseech. Let wisdom guide you to build relationships suitable to the journey of life you aspire. Respect the order of life and you shall be fruitful and multiply exceedingly!

Six Points to Remember Along the Journey

- Go to those who are established for years in whatever you want to do, having accountability for integrity of the heart.

- Ask people questions about themselves for them to talk and give you things necessary for your journey.

- Create relationships from caring to ask more about them.

- Have more connection with communication to establish relationship.

- Personal standards of excellence comes as you raise your level of discipline, people become attracted to you

Unity is the key of abundance and success

The labor of six days is given to build a legacy of provision. By nature, a man is not designed equally to a woman. Man has the greater responsibility of the two as the keeper of the earth. Man is given authority to govern the life he secures, protects, and watches over. The absence of a man from a family makes life very hard on a woman who was not made to bear the burdens of the family. She loses the high nurturer's energy to one of exhaustion. However, the one who endures much shall receive much. The order of creation, naked in nature is of an abundant life. Those of royalty have a dominion where life is governed judiciously. Like lions the pride is blameless from threat of scarcity as lionesses caress and nurture the young for a father's legacy. How may a family rest if captivity brings about conflict? Unable to look beyond the paradigm of society many lose hope to sobriety that rules in favor of royal legacy. Respect the order of life and you shall be fruitful and multiply exceedingly!

Having an order for a way of life not bound by captivity makes free the children to inherit and see the importance of legacy. The study of a father's house, a master builder of success, looks beyond the daily needs of necessity into areas dark and glorious for counsel of all times. Only can he be the guardian protector of many souls. A sagacious woman calls from earth her destiny to console her victory. Royal seed is called out of her womb, who follows the order of life prepared for a master builder to cultivate noble succession for a better tomorrow. Respect the order of life and you shall be fruitful and multiply exceedingly!

The transfer of ancestral knowledge is the possession of royal descent to perfect the ways of business, a way of life in the physical, spiritual realm prior to any union. A search for identity remains a mystery of many held in captivity, working endlessly to make ends meet. Life seems good not to worry about what one does not know. What fate does one have in the future being complacent in society? The captivity of us all. If there is no plan of action to accomplish a vision, how shall one make provision for legacy? Therefore, not all are lions by nature of royal descent to serve and be served as a family of unity. Respect the order of life and you shall be fruitful and multiply exceedingly!

Walk with grace knowing that you're vision of life is to become a beneficiary of a divine monarchy. Blessed are they who bless one another and encourage love throughout the land to preserve decency, a discipline of a clean conscience and sound mind. Whatever you give do so without any expectation of what you shall receive; for doing so your blessings shall overtake you being greater than the dream conceived. And in the end the love you take is unequivocal to the love you make. Respect the order of life and you shall be fruitful and multiply exceedingly!

Cleverness Guards the Establishment

The things within reach capture it while you have it within your presence; even if the outcome of sacrifice is greater than the consequence of action. Protect the resources as you are able to wisely maneuver the tools of the trade. Escape or withdraw from any circumstance of great risk while time is on your side. Never leave things in a mess. The last impression is to be done with grace so that your reputation follows you.

There's something about being a king that is so noble to be true to self regardless of feeling felt for others. To give into feeling of wrongdoings weakens the divine nature of regency. There can be sympathy for wrongdoing not even of the poor. No favor of status shall be looked upon of a person's trespass or transgression; but shall be acknowledged to put an end to sin. Transgression and trespass shall not be hidden from plain sight or in the action it is transpired. What is exposed of the deed done, zero tolerance strikes out what remains under the sun.

A Royal Heart

What makes up a heart of royalty? Knowing what was and will be done is for the greater good of humanity instead of vanity? Having the foresight to see beyond? That's when the natures of the heart are at play. A man has four natures as does the heart has four chambers for the circulation of oxygen throughout the body. These four chambers connect man to the universe in which he lives. Every action stored with emotion is in the heart. The heart's makeup is the law of attraction to radiate electromagnetic energy of what is stored and desired. Who can know the heart of man? Unless the heart be known by experience, it could be deceitful if not dealt with truthfully. The energy of all mankind is within the heart. Mind over matter should be examined carefully in consideration of the heart. Whatever a man thinks he shall become. Any action without the heart takes one off course not to fulfill destiny. A heart of stone resists kinetic energy for the room of potential only.

A royal heart comes from a source of purity that illuminates the state of the mind known as your passion for integrity. This respected love of yourself is true happiness, the most valued of all attributes for clarity. Happiness brings clarity to life to make decisions void of confusion as it searches out the truest intentions to honor values. The upkeep of happiness depends upon the surrounding influences that may subject you to tolerate things outside values. Happiness is a force that must be acted upon in all situations to do whatsoever is right according to integrity of values as it guides and moves one to royal heart. The royal heart is impenetrable to evil and cannot abide in or with it nor allow the authority of oppression to succeed. A royal heart has an ethical concern for all to live in equity and peace.

The nobility of a royal heart drives oppression away from the land. Whomever is not concerned with the wellbeing of others could there be true happiness? This matter raises a flag as to what honor a man or woman shall have.

Statements can imply honor as actions create the outlook of values lived. Honor is bestowed upon a record of service proven trustworthy in deed. A commitment of trust that secures the work chosen of service endows honor. Words spoken in agreement, by oath, or among the presence of others, contingent upon goodwill; if not consummated dishonors the one who reneges the occasion of words spoken in agreement. Generally, one's performance is scaled upon the nature of events encountered. The most favorable outcome is the honor bestowed upon one at agreement than one who does not always follow through fully as intended to be outside of goodwill.

Merit is given among those whose quality of service is beyond exceptional. The respect to honor an agreement and to accomplish all without fuss is a preferred merit that distinguishes those relationships that are highly valuable. The respect of consideration found in the heart of those who choose not to ignore others is honorable. Any thoughts that are devalued and not taken in consideration can deteriorate a friendship. A friend will contribute what is appreciated, but if what is offered is not attributed to appreciation; can there be room for consideration?

In some cases, many are forced to take on things of no appreciation for the sake of friendship. The intrinsic value of friendship does not let down the emotion of another. Yet, this idea of friendship does not reveal one's true identity by a form of obligation to another. A false sense of value may stem from a suppressed feeling of a situational weakening in the friendship. Consideration finds appreciation to be called a friend of merit and not by the duty that obligates.

There's a force that can create a new phenomenon as many marvel at the synergy of light beheld in its beauty known as a great relationship. All have a choice in establishing beautiful relationships as colorful thoughts are inclusive of one another and not exclusive to differences. Many relationships that are short lived moments of life can be referred to as interim. Whereas interrupt relationships can reconvene after separation to a continuous relationship contingent upon amended grounds or boundaries never to be broken. Each relationship is precious and not to be diminished as the life cherished is as treasure forever.

However, there are those relationships that seek not a royal heart that are for a season. The unselfish experiences go far beyond the existence of what was thought impossible. A relationship that is continuous in what is shared and appreciated is invaluable lasting for a lifetime. The universal law of making peace promotes a continuous relationship to thrive without the force of disruption. Clarity is the key to maintain a royal heart, therefore be happy in this game of life.

There are four natures of man that evolve from the heart. A man's heart is impressionable as a child large as can be learning to take the right action. However, self-preservation is not exemplified one will please others instead of doing what's right for the happiness of moral values. Childhood is where the heart is formed, the first nature that oversees all other natures of man. A joyful heart is playful and happy to know there is balance a balance to life that to be at peace with self and others. Man is the guardian of peace and protector of the woman's feelings. Family gives a child the experience to know the feelings of the heart to express it with dignity.

A man has the right to resent anyone forcing him against his will. The state of mind a man chooses determines whether his conduct frees him of the dreadful thing placed upon him. A man's conduct reflects his peace. The state of a man's peace has not been tried fully until he has adventured the trials of life. A man who strives to overcome all obstacles through righteousness will fear no evil to confront or circumvent it.

The roles of a man's heart are learned of his family or inherently passed down as he seeks to know his position in each relationship. The craft of man that keeps him active is his pursuit of passion like no other creation it brings him happiness. The first nature of man a woman must know what inspires him to do more. Vice versa.

The second nature of man watches to observe things with his heart to know when to be on a prowl with a lion like passion burning from within. Nothing can overcome it. The third nature of man is unity, learned of within or without family he searches for values that connects him with the hearts of others. Knowing that there is much success in unity, a man has a strong commitment to recognize those who lookout for one another. The same nature is of cape buffaloes on wild on plains of Africa.

The forth-nature of man is the fight of survival that delivers himself and any oppressed by means of justification as he shows mercy to those in need. His heart is on the watch for intelligence to know who, what, when, where, and how things are happening. This nature is similar to the eagle who never takes uncalculated risks.

Depending on the circumstances faced a man for good reason will remain within his nature in respect of his environment if he does not have the foresight see beyond.

Over time false emotions appearing real cloud the heart and mind. We need healing to move on to be great successful people in which we dream. Therefore, we cleanse both heart and mind in silence to enter a meditative state that works out the nature of our heart. The inner heart has intuitive intelligence for a transformational plan to guide us. The manifestation of growth exists when an idea is formed in the heart for our dreams become a reality. It is our destiny to know our passion. Test the truth to know what's real.

Align yourself with people that can help you overcome fears and troubles of the past that you to bless others. Value is a transference of trust, driven by things other than a person's self-gain. People are habitual and habits are required for them to function. We place value on what we spend. A commitment to life is expressed in actions you take and behaviors you express. Make decisions where you are safe before you venture out in the world. A trusted group allows you to learn in your vulnerability. If one's ambitions of optimism and faith makes another uncomfortable to doubt, then the disparity between them is out of scope to build. Don't let bad habits devalue your dreams. You must trust with belief until you have done it to take to the world.

The Clarity of Keen Judgment

When did a decision become crucial and was it emotional? We are all born with decisions made for us until the time comes when we shall make our own. However, when those decisions were made for us, we were not emotional behind them, why now? Decisions from the heart may factor in some difficulty, but the skill of questioning to query the answer helps to bring out the truth is logic. Careful observation and meditation are the antidote approach to why things occurred for so long. There is now no need to blame or feel sorrow for the grievance felt; when you have done it to yourself, you dread never to go back to that predicament. Keen judgment is non-emotional as it searches to seek out the truth of a matter revealed by wisdom of logic.

The quality of decision making impacts the quality of relationships. Setting aside time to secretly place your thoughts refocuses energy to renew self-value. The ability to quite the mind, body, and soul allows room to do the unthinkable, even the release of love to forgive what was unforgiveable. Establishing values in written form helps to explore the nature of consciousness sensitive to morality and beliefs of self and others. Stimulate the conscience for familiarity of morality and beliefs as well as to avoid distractions by creating a plan of action that identifies personal and private thoughts to be shared with those of familiarity.

A viewpoint, circumstance, or belief is to be respected and not forced. A healthy mind improves with time the belief for a more favorable result. Change the belief for success when something is the prison of confusion. What naturally is logical, the truth, and probable may not be accepted by most but whoever applies it shall succeed.

A proactive persona expresses thoughts and makes decisions to do what is valued for growth and good will. A reactive persona does not take responsibility for actions to reflect what is of value. Life becomes stagnant from unresolved issues, stuck in the lower self of negative emotional pride. A fulfillment of growth comes when from self-love and forgiveness of offenses suffered from those of the past. Encouragement yields ownership of all power through what you love rather than hate. Perception is a limited perspective of life, nonetheless we learn from one another to embrace the power of the moment from all beliefs that makes you free. Freedom is the way of a child to do whatsoever makes the soul full of happiness. Limitations grows from society's view to not do what makes up feel free. One must lose mind over matter to gain back that pure heart of awareness as the body becomes one with the subconscious mind. If you exercise to have fun, the body's muscles will loosen up to relax the mind to speak the language of the subconscious in what you do for that imagery to become the association at work. Sound logic yields power for good fortune when endorsed in what is loved. Therefore, let mercy, truth, and happiness be the universal law that governs moral values and beliefs for what you do.

Test the truth to know what's real. Know the impact of what you are doing to walk in truth. Assert your right to point out the wrong. Know who you are and shake things up when there's no accountability of behavior. It's all on you to guard your heart and mind and I yield.

The Clarity of Will Power

What is clarity when it comes to the heart and mind? Clarity is your gut feeling of what you know to do right. That gut feeling if not performed later becomes grievous in the heart. When you feel what you are saying in confidence of who you are as you express ideas you have; clarity is the agreement of the heart and mind for will power to grow. Will Power is the esteem of who you are to do anything in life. There is will power in everything we do, however the will power of an open mind of expansion for new ideas finds its place in that of business. Business is the ingenuity of the heart to have knowledge of self-worth in alignment with destiny. The happier you are doing something, will power increases exponentially by the number of hours necessary for perfection to attain mastery. Stay true to yourself and do not let others get in the way of your progression as you build will power you shall have clarity to focus on realistic goals of importance you can feel within your heart and mind.

Cloudy judgment is the result of external influences that do not produce that gut feeling.

Take control of judgment to build a new paradigm based on truth.

Stop thinking of the external situations to focus solely on self.

Otherwise, one creates problems that are not there and do not matter. Solve problems, ask questions, and eliminate all inappropriate truths. Creative logic brings forth happiness with more money to spend.

Eventually, a lack of will power can result from undesirable situations that alter attitude negatively. Such situations of loneliness, depression, fear, and addiction can easily alter one's attitude to doubt or experience anxiety. Sleep deprivation is another situation caused mostly by a lack of discipline. The importance of discipline maintains homeostasis, balance within the human respiratory system. When the body sleeps at night, the human brain regulates sugar throughout the body during its resting period of at least seven hours for the mental state to be fully alert. The will power can be made strong by eating every so often as needed after awakening from sleep to a morning yawn and stretch. This is why the physical body is in direct correlation to the spirit of the body to have clarity is strong will power.

The main discipline of the physical body is exercise and nutrition for the increase of self-esteem and strength of immune system. Exercise is beneficial in the morning as the will power is full, one is less likely to make impulse decisions. The number of breaths exhaled is a testament of full will power to know one's potential.

Overcome the lack of will power with exercise, music, friends, meditation, or whatever that makes you happy. The imagination, conscience, and will power together are the order of sovereignty that is inherent of life. The internal power of a person influences one's sovereignty.

A vision of the end begins imagination for purpose of identity and association that life is created twice in the spiritual (mental) and physical (corporeal) plane. Whatever you want help people without compensation and things will work in your favor.

The beginning of each day is like a set of divine instructions for the execution of synergy. Having the end in mind to share a common vision with a group that owns a since of guidance to influence decisions by mutual trust.

Avoid stagnant behavior, be on the prowl for new insight to stay aligned to the goal. Remember to feed your heart from thoughts occupied in continuous improvement. Chaos and disorder surfaces from an imbalanced lifestyle which has no time for self and is insensitive to other aspects of life. Usually, the preoccupation of something neglects the other areas of life, if not balanced with self-preservation. Therefore, self-preservation allows room for will power to grow with clarity to execute the true desires of the heart. Take good care of yourself!

Clarity Activates Energy

Sometimes no matter what you try to focus on, nothing seems to work. Any unresolved issue hinders the maximum potential of new creative energy. Once resolved one's energy is free to create and if not stagnant to do nothing. Commonly, the focus of attention that many place attributes upon are seen of the eyes rather than of personality. A proactive personality deals with things sensibly and realistically in a practical manner having an awareness of responsibility. A proactive choice is an optimistic approach over a pessimistic outcome to govern the right attitude in situations one cannot control. This approach is healthy for positive growth an encouragement of happiness. On the other hand, a pessimistic approach can result in a dysfunctional behavior that complains, argues, resents, and etc. without taking responsibility and/or identifying the root issue of the cause. Signs of negativity should be avoided as much as possible for it is unhealthy for progression. The outcome always is predicated on the response of attitude, which warrants the freedom one chooses.

The right attitude awakens self-conscious to a new awareness that visions of destiny can be seen afore-time through the scrutiny of predicaments forced beyond one's control. The only control is what options one is limited. The unfamiliar will appear to be strange even to entertain strangers. The only thing one thinks is strange is what is seen within self that does not agree with others.

The noblest quality of highest value a human can experience in life is to choose the right response in search of peace for all situations.

Harmonize the energy of relationships by placing the order of things which matters most ahead of things of less significance. The harmony of energy sought out of relationships is opposed to task mastering tasks. Instead, relationships driven by values that lead direction as time is reciprocal of the energy invested creates harmony. Discipline helps to manage efficiency as prioritization remains a focus of relationship.

The mind over matter concept is mental, yet spiritual. Thoughts must be filtered properly to not be overwhelmed with excessive information. Withdrawal symptoms may occur after one is removed from an environment for a period of time to limit distractions. Expand the mind of concentration by reading, writing, and thinking consciously to sharpen values and emotional intelligence to gain back control. The expression of thought in words is considered an art of intelligence that stimulates the mind for continuous improvement.

The seclusion of the mind helps to deal with adversities of great circumstances. All stress violates the space occupied of the conscience. The management of stress is mental as it defines the sense of purpose, values, and ability to cope with the realities of life personally and environmentally.

The Clarity of Influence

How is your influence within your family, friends, peers, and professional occupation?

Clarity helps to stay focused on the main point without distractions, so everyone knows it's important to listen when it's time for an answer. People are usually influenced in these areas of favor (esteemed by others), reputation, and significant contributions. Bring purpose to what you want to move beyond limitations into an environment of success that responds favorably. Highly valued is the ability to process what you know to use when ready; discernment is necessary to process information and end up with results unfulfilled. The truth as an appropriate response will always be a good result, as the wrong or inappropriate answer is never good enough. Shared experiences based on unseemly facts can lead people to bad results.

Social influence happens spontaneously from sharing and receiving others' feelings of mutual appreciation and acceptance are the motivation. Generally, once a need is satisfied, there is no motivation. Influence can be a tool for understanding another by accepting to know their world and that their values matter to you emotionally and physically to feel the warmth of sacred human communication. A cooperative state of mind does not listen to the other's awareness but makes things efficient by demand. This condition of not listening from another's frame of reference devalues a relationship. Selecting the right channel of influence to enter another's world of thinking without getting lost is an effort of admirable skill.

However, if there is an inability to identify the depths of thought, it is wise to avoid getting too involved to lose control. Wisdom does not risk vulnerability, whereas one cannot accomplish much. Having accumulative knowledge within context; helps to know the frame of reference for filtering a reality of an unknown world.

A teachable relationship for social growth without stereotypes to share ideas with others is an inspiration. A noble character creates energy within all relationships. The integrity of creative cooperation allows for a mutual vision, respect, and understanding to occur below ground before shooting upwards. The higher degree of indoctrination the more obedient the slave. The ego showcases the level of obedience to rationalize its paradigm too afraid to embrace the true identity of self for a new way of life. Don't be afraid to create your own destiny nor insult your intelligence to be treated as a child by others esteemed.

Nurture all relationships in your life morally and socially so that courage excels. It is nobler to focus attention on one than to labor for the masses. Discipline activates the mind to balance the body's emotions and the spirit's energy. Nurturing and affirming one another activates the mind to create synergy. A broken relationship requires empathy, patience, and care of concern; therefore, choose wisely if it is the one that matters. A seed planted may appear on the outside to have what it needs, yet the seed, without the nourishment of concern internally, will not flourish to yield desirable fruit.

Synergy, the communication of multiplication is not spent on adversarial wasted efforts. The realization of synergy is that there is no esteem in conflict and in its simplest form the whole is greater than the sum. Synergy is connected to a sense of direction that knows no bounds of obstruction and prevents internal conflict from being reactive.

Compromise does not synergize, but trust for a dynamic way of life is created without ego. The dynamic way of life creates alternatives to meet each other's needs together without force. Valued differences are the creative energy where strength lies within a common vision and value system. Inclusion without separation brings about relaxation in an optimistic empathy that secures people to understand.

The synergy of moral differences solves problems exponentially in new ways. Intelligence is ignorance if used to control the minds of people who look to be told what to do rather than encourage alternatives. Having options not only allows one to view things differently, but is healthy for growth in development of choice.

Clarity brings the Success of Support

How successful do you feel? The desire to do the unthinkable or unimagined has much to do with esteem. Experience can boost esteem to drive success in any particular area of our lives. However, when things are in disarray, the mind has clutter, and the more unresolved relationships, the more chatter or further away one is from clarity. Success is the ability to process what you know. Our esteem plays a big part in our happiness. The feeling of happiness must be tied to success. We learn to do what it is we like. Progression feels good, and so does a sense of accomplishment to be relieved. It can be very difficult to gain the support of others by wheeling those around you into something undesired.

Search for your passion and concentrate all efforts in that direction. Secure the things identified as most important by choice of activity done well to produce extraordinary results. Clarity organizes resources for what is needed to support the vision created. The power of attraction wields a consistent force from an effort to a team of unity. Consistency is a key component of values not compromised in the creation of successful relationships. A mutual benefit of respect creates wealth as it overlooks competition as a distraction. Failure prohibits consistency as it does not continue to exceed one's maximum potential that fear becomes a factor of a fallen state of anxiety. Another obstacle to support success is the thought that leeches on the energy of others for control as one is drenched in ego.

A belief attached to a character forms ego for the projection of a fictitious character instead of one's true self. True creativity synergizes differences, the ability to see the problem differently from many vantage points allows for the increase of knowledge and power to excel beyond normal circumstances. Though irreconcilable differences do not allow one to reach the capacity to create in abundance, competition may be the arena of sport entertained not collaborate of success for support. Success is a progressive realization of self-worth.

Living A Successful Happy Life on Earth: Nuggets of Wisdom

In the vibrant mosaic of life, where experiences intertwine like threads of joy, the wisdom bestowed upon us by our elders becomes a radiant beacon. It lights up the journey to a truly joyous and satisfying existence on Earth. As we joyfully navigate the intricacies of relationships, career choices, and the pursuit of happiness, the shared insights from those who have danced through life's diverse chapters become priceless treasures. From the depths of their experiences, the elders offer a perspective that goes beyond the ordinary definitions of success. It is within this timeless pool of wisdom that we unearth the keys to a life brimming with purpose, connection, and unbridled joy. Take heed to these values for a beautiful and happy life:

1. Happiness is Your Responsibility: Take charge of your own happiness and well-being throughout the time of your life.

2. Key to a Satisfying Marriage: Finding a partner with a similar upbringing, general orientation, and values is crucial for a long and fulfilling marriage, despite the value society places on diversity.

3. Practical Guidance from Elders: Continue seeking wisdom from elders for a unique perspective on the "good life" in contemporary society.

4. Partner Focus in Relationships: Start your day by asking, "What can I do for my partner?" Foster a mindset of giving without keeping score.

5. Wealth Isn't Everything: Pursuing wealth for the sake of possessions and status doesn't lead to happiness or success, according to those who have lived longer.

6. Interpersonal Skills Matter: Regardless of talent or brilliance, success hinges on interpersonal skills.

7. Autonomy in Career: Career satisfaction involves having the autonomy to make decisions and pursue interests without excessive control from above.

8. Family Time, No Regrets: Elders emphasize the importance of spending quality time with your children, as it becomes a source of cherished memories.

9. Shared Activities and Sacrifices: Meaningful memories come from shared activities and the willingness to make sacrifices for quality time with loved ones.

As we reflect upon the collective wisdom bestowed upon us by our elders, we unearth the profound truths that form the foundation of a successful life on Earth. The essence lies not in the relentless pursuit of material wealth or conformity to societal expectations but in the intricate dance of relationships, the embrace of autonomy, and the cultivation of cherished memories.

Embarking on an exhilarating adventure, the ageless revelations woven into the intricate threads of their lives call us to prioritize the essence of existence: forging meaningful connections, embracing genuine happiness, and savoring the shared moments that weave the very fabric of our being. As we heed the echoes of the past, our expedition unfolds towards a life drenched in purpose, authenticity, and the resounding echoes of a genuinely triumphant earthly odyssey.

An Intimate Union
of Relationship

A Woman for Man

Why is a man good for a woman and a woman good for a man? Is it true that men know nothing about woman's hearts? Perhaps a man could benefit from a woman. Is she agreeable and searching for information to know herself, even to share comfort and happiness? Should a woman let a man's behavior be the root of hers? She is never so important in a man's eye than her Father's. If the absence of his presence does not abide, can she know how to treat a man even to confide? What inducements would she have to marry? Excluding fortune and position, why would a man want her to enlist in his affairs without knowing the capability of supporting him? How can a woman know a man's heart without the return of affection? Would a man intentionally give a woman an idea of how he feels than he does? The best way is to be strait forward without controversy. Let it be spoken, plainly felt as words melt away whatever ails the pain of inquiry today.

Principles of
Marriage

The Woman

What roles have a woman learned of her life to be true to herself? Nature consists of balance throughout all creation roles help to balance the life we aspire to live. How does a woman know if she ready to embrace engagement? Is her heart made ready for an unselfish union?

Prior to any union of a man and woman taking place, it is wise for a woman to consider how she is to build her home by knowing what happened to those fallen. The nurturer of the home is an art of science much appreciated in healing and comforting. The woman is the great communicator to address all needs of the home without any issue of insecurity. Having first learned of her elders, she is active in her community to help those in need. Especially, when it comes to the children, she helps to maintain a loving and respectable home; well-balanced of order, kindness, and full of patience. A teacher who's always learning to fill the home with wonderful things to bring excitement of new opportunities to see a new universe from the one envisioned of her past or inspired of life efforts. Diligently, she seeks out knowledge to address matters socially for conscious decisions economically and politically that may impact the home environmentally.

Healthy counsel of older women before marriage is a great advantage for preparing a woman's heart for entering a covenant of union. A firm relationship of order and discipline with her father of love and respect helps to ensure that his authority is transferred respectfully to the man of marriage. The woman can attest to the ways a man learned of her father and any exposure received from her family. The parental development of an unbiased relationship alongside siblings of no partiality in love allows for a woman to be a cheerful giver of love and comfort. However, without a healthy upbringing, a woman must reveal the missing pieces of her heart to make life complete. Knowledge of self comes from many hours searching for the work that brings clarity to life for everlasting happiness within the self that is apparent. Nature reflects the work created by a greater life force for all to witness creativity from a sense of inner peace. A woman who is honest in knowing herself and not insecure by the esteem of others but diligently searches for self-worth for the sake of happiness shall be rewarded with the respect of the good company. Watching and praying is the course of action a woman can recognize the energy that appreciates the essence of character she has become to know her mate has arrived. The perfection of beauty is present as each stand in awe of the other, sensing a connection to be one on earth. Marriage is not for all, but for those willing to sacrifice all they know for a new universe to be discovered. A great deal of consideration must always be made on account of others' well-being.

A conscientious woman is desirable not in dating, but in character no matter who's in her presence. A woman who displaces love cannot nurture the home as love is not the affection that comes from dating. The love is inherent to existence of life. This love is unbiased, forgiving, and merciful with common sense not to hold on to the past for resentment even to grudge carry.

The woman of abuse is less fortunate than a woman of no history. Consequently, she must revisit all circumstances of abuse to ensure not only a new relationship will allow growth; but a healthy one with valuable insight for the security of her thoughts. Otherwise, any unresolved issues may revisit her thoughts to haunt with suspicion and unexpectedly cause disruption or even destroy the foundation of the union.

A woman lacking the love necessary to be whole (secure) throughout life may be very needy, depending upon others for her issues quite often than most. Whenever a woman cannot receive the love she expects, as things may take a wrong course of action, she may resort to an addiction to fulfill her void. She makes promises to improve but finds it quite difficult to honor what she has agreed. Often at times, she is unhappy with whoever does not give in to her demand as she conceives an imaginary situation of things for a false pretense.

The aforementioned is a depiction of an insecure woman who may destroy a marriage as she puts her desires above others' needs doing as she pleases. This is the unhidden act of selfishness not seen on the surface; but in the sight of those of a more intimate relationship. Any hidden selfishness is a sign of immaturity. Hopefully, the man engaged discovers this before he enters a covenant of union to prevent such grievance of emotional distress.

Beautiful is it to find one whom you can share your heart without circumspection. A priceless treasure is secured from all issues without the hassle of worry to weary one in inquiries of uncertainty. The heart and mind are the most prized possession beyond the looks of beauty. You can do so much more than one can imagine with another who is after the heart and mind to be in alignment with the direction you pursue throughout life. The reflection of one's attitude is an attest to aptitude to discover and resolve issues in the course of action consciously and ignorantly.

A beautiful heart and mind give you so much liberty to do the impossible that it makes life very easy to make provisions for others in need of vital resources. Hearts of great joy and satisfaction elevate at higher level of communication beyond the vows of commitment and promise. A quantum leap into an irresistible love that never imagines departure. Consideration for one another is a major component of love that allows this union to become a reality as one diligently seeks and confess faults and character flaws. Welcoming rebuke from anyone who rightfully has been wronged in an encounter of offense.

The beloved is loved in every way possible knowing that the merit of life given is to the works seen of the heart and mind of matters to avoid all selfishness from one's existence. Now is it mentioned and seen as a vibrant unity that there is nothing impossible that cannot be done.

A Wife: A Sacred Partner in Her Husband's Authority

The Honored Position of a Wife

In the realm of life's intricate tapestry, both man and woman are entrusted with multifarious roles. However, nestled within the fabric of a woman's existence lies her paramount duty as a wife—a calling bestowed upon her by the divine hand. Such is the essence of her original purpose, ordained by the celestial proclamation.

"And Yah said, 'It is not good that the man should be alone; I will make him a help meet for him.'" (Genesis 2:18)

This sacred verse unveils the profound truth that the role of a wife eclipses even that of a mother. Undeniably, the role of motherhood bears immense significance, yet it springs forth from and thrives within the sacred ministry of being a "help meet." Let it be known that this does not diminish the worth of a single woman. If, in His infinite wisdom, Yah summons an adult woman to embrace a life of singularity—be it for a season or in perpetuity—He, in His divine providence, assumes the mantle of her Husband.

Behold, there exists a distinction between a wife and a virgin. The unwedded woman diligently attends to the affairs of the Most High God, aspiring to embody holiness in both body and spirit... (1 Corinthians 7:34)

A wife is holy and remains pure in marital intimacy. The essence of a virgin's holiness lies in consecration unto the Most High God, signifying a complete separation. In other words an unmarried woman is wholly consecrated to the divine as a wife is consecrated to her husband.

Now, let us delve into the profound ministry and purpose of a wife. She is beckoned to be her husband's helper, for without her, his ministry shall remain incomplete. She stands as an indispensable pillar within the holy marital union, an integral component of the divine partnership forged by the heavens. She must grasp the vision entrusted to her husband, acknowledging her role within its grand tapestry. In bringing the Most High God's vision to fruition, a woman of godliness assumes a position of authority and reverence within the sphere of influence in which they are placed.

In my pursuit of an ideal life partner, my heart resonates with the vision of an exceptional entrepreneurial woman who embodies a rich tapestry of qualities. She possesses an innate understanding of her own identity and a remarkable ability to channel her passion into profitable ventures, mirroring my own aspirations. Our connection transcends the boundaries of conventional relationships; it's a profound love story rooted in shared values, a profound appreciation for the quality of life enriched by abundance, and an unwavering commitment to freedom culture, family, heritage, and a legacy that touches the lives of generations to come.

This extraordinary woman, who stands as a paragon of beauty both inside and out, seamlessly resonates with the depths of my mind and the core of my soul. Her alignment with a higher purpose is palpable in her unwavering reverence for humanity and her resolute adherence to unwavering moral principles. She radiates a magnetic aura that speaks of regal elegance, which is underlined by her commitment to cleanliness and a refined aesthetic in both her personal appearance and her living spaces.

In the realm of relationships, she extends her warmth and grace to friends and companions, using her highly developed communication skills to connect on deep and meaningful levels. As a steadfast champion of freedom culture, she believes in the liberation of not only herself but also those she holds dear. Her devotion to family and heritage is unwavering, and she carries a sense of legacy that promises to leave an indelible mark on the lives of countless souls for generations to come.

Much like an immortal royal queen, her presence carries an air of timeless magnificence. Her commitment to making a lasting impact on the world sets her apart, embodying qualities that transcend the limitations of time. Together, our destinies intertwine as we craft a life that mirrors the grandeur of our aspirations. With each passing day, our connection grows stronger, fueled by a love that knows no bounds. Our shared journey is one of boundless joy, enduring success, and a love that echoes through the ages.

What Are Some of a Wife's Responsibilities?

First and foremost, a wife must embody the role of a counselor, seeking counsel from YAH offering to her husband wisdom sought out for life and resources to live out the best human experience. As history narrates, Eve herself served as a counselor to Adam, yet the advice she tendered was cloaked in malevolence. Although Adam recognized the counsel's malice, he regrettably succumbed to its allure. A parallel tale unfolds in the annals of Ahab and Jezebel, their nefarious partnership bearing testament to the immense influence a woman holds over her husband's decisions—for better or worse. It may so happen that a wife finds herself unable to articulate the reasons behind her convictions concerning a course of action. In such instances, a husband ought to regard his wife's advice with utmost seriousness. For it is through pride that many a husband has spurned the counsel of his marital companion, only to face grievous financial or personal loss.

"And the angel came in unto her, and said, 'Hail, thou that art highly favored, the Most High God is with thee: blessed art thou among women.'" (Luke 1:28)

It is noteworthy that Yah, prior to confiding in Joseph, chose to divulge the impending arrival of the Messiah to a woman destined to become his wife—Mary. A parallel scenario unfolds within the pages of Judges 13, wherein the Angel of the Most High God first appeared to the wife, rather than her husband. In the face of Manoah's trepidation upon receiving the revelation of the Most High God, his marriage partner—the beacon of his life—was able to assuage his fears with wisdom and logic.

"And Manoah said unto his wife, 'We shall surely die, because we have seen the Most High God.' But his wife said unto him, 'If the Most High God were pleased to kill us, he would not have received a burnt offering and a meat offering at our hands, neither would he have shown us all these things, nor would as at this time have told us such things as these.'" (Judges 13:22-23)

In this exemplary exchange between Manoah and his wife, we witness the profound influence a wife wields over her husband's spiritual journey. As he grappled with the weight of divine revelation, it was his wife—the embodiment of wisdom and faith—who guided him through his doubts and fears. Together, they stood as a testament to the sacred bond and partnership bestowed upon them by the Most High God.

Thus, in the tapestry of marital life, a wife's responsibilities extend far beyond the confines of a single role. She is a counselor, a confidant, and a guiding light. She is a vessel through which the wisdom and grace of the Most High God can flow into her husband's life. Let every husband heed the words of his wife, for in her insights lies the potential for blessings and guidance that surpass human understanding.

May these words, penned by the humble scribe Sir Justus Abramelech, illuminate the profound depths of a wife's calling and inspire all who read them to cherish and honor the sacred partnership between husband and wife, under the watchful gaze of the Most High God.

As a counselor, it is imperative for a wife to cultivate and nurture her relationship with the Most High God and deepen her knowledge of His Word. Likewise, the husband should prioritize his communion with YAH, for he stands directly under the guidance of Yeshua. Often, a woman possesses a heightened spiritual sensitivity, a divine blessing, yet also a potential peril. This is one of the reasons why she must willingly submit to her husband's leadership. Moreover, she can expand her knowledge in specific areas that are likely to provide valuable counsel to her husband.

"For favor is deceitful, and beauty is vain: but a woman that feareth the Most High God, she shall be praised." (Proverbs 31:30)

Additionally, a wife serves as a helper, assisting her husband in fulfilling YAH's mission for their lives. Within the bounds of her husband's authority, she possesses her own sphere of influence. Together, as a unified team, the two marriage partners are called to serve Yeshua and align their purpose accordingly.

The Woman of Noble Character

In the ancient wisdom of Proverbs 31, we find a timeless portrayal of a wife fulfilling her divine purpose. It is important to recognize that each person possesses unique talents and abilities. The essence lies in the partnership, diligence, and unwavering commitment, rather than prescribing specific occupations such as real estate or business. So, let us explore the profound aspects that define an honorable wife.

Let us uncover the valuable traits displayed by an honorable wife within the text:

1. She is of immeasurable value to her husband—more precious than any other person or possession in the world. Countless husbands have disregarded or overlooked this incredible gift from YAH, leading to the loss or harm of their marital union. A holy woman is a treasure to be pursued [Proverbs 12:4, 18:22, 19:14], and if a woman desires a holy husband, she must ensure she embodies the qualities such men seek.

2. She is a paragon of trustworthiness. Her husband can confidently engage in his work or attend to other aspects of life, knowing that he can entrust her with their affairs. Indeed, the knowledge that she faithfully and skillfully fulfills her duties fosters a remarkable partnership. Their union is one founded on trust, mutual support, and shared responsibilities. With each partner embracing their roles with dedication and competence, they form a formidable team, working hand in hand to navigate the challenges of life. The husband finds solace in knowing that his wife is committed to their shared goals, while the wife takes pride in her ability to contribute effectively to their collective endeavors. Together, they exemplify the essence of a harmonious and fruitful partnership, where each partner's diligence and competence enhance the strength and success of their union. Whether engaged in her own endeavors, he has the utmost confidence that she is always striving to benefit their union utilizing time and resources wisely, always giving her best. Proverbs 31:11-12 bears witness to her unwavering fidelity.

3. She is unafraid of hard work to provide for her family. If her abilities do not lie in the art of garment-making, she diligently seeks out fine attire from reputable establishments. Recognizing her limitations, she explores alternative avenues to provide her family with garments of commendable quality. Instead of being disheartened by her lack of skill, she displays resourcefulness by scouring second-hand stores for clothing that meets her standards. She understands that while new garments may be desirable, practicality and prudence necessitate seeking the best options for her husband and family within their means. In this manner, she demonstrates her commitment to fulfilling her role as a provider and caretaker, ensuring that her loved ones are well-clothed and cared for. She exhibits creativity in obtaining the best for her husband and family at a reasonable cost, especially when financial constraints arise. (Proverbs 31:13, 19, 27)

4. She possesses wisdom in matters of food and resource management. She knows where to find the best sales and understands the cost-effectiveness of traveling from store to store. Furthermore, she places great importance on procuring nourishing sustenance for the well-being of her family. Recognizing the significance of a balanced and wholesome diet, she devotes her attention to selecting and preparing food that promotes their health and vitality. With a discerning eye, she seeks out food options that are not only appetizing but also rich in nutrients. She understands that proper nourishment is a foundation for physical well-being and endeavors to provide her loved ones with meals that support their growth and vitality. Her commitment to ensuring the health of her family reflects her dedication as a conscientious and caring wife, demonstrating her profound understanding of the significance of nutrition in their lives. (Proverbs 31:14, 18)

These principles, woven into the tapestry of a holy wife's character, exemplify the virtues that are worthy of admiration and praise. May all who read these words, scribed by the humble Sir Justus Abramelech, glean wisdom and inspiration, embracing the profound beauty and significance of a wife's role in accordance with the Most High God's design.

Continuing with the profound insights penned by Sir Justus Abramelech, we delve into additional facets of an honorable wife's character:

5. She diligently cares for all those under her wing, ensuring fairness in their treatment. Her compassion and care extend beyond the boundaries of her own household, revealing a heart that beats with a deep sense of justice and fairness. She is not content with solely attending to the needs of her family, but she also takes a keen interest in the well-being of those around her. She is mindful of the injustices that exist in the world and seeks to make a positive impact in the lives of others. (Proverbs 31:15, 21) Her example serves as a beacon of hope, inspiring others to embrace the values of compassion and justice. In a world where self-interest often prevails, she stands as a shining testament to the transformative power of a heart that beats for justice.

6. Possessing astute business (entrepreneurial) acumen to contribute to the well-being of her family, she knows how to generate a fair profit. She understands the importance of self-sufficiency and takes pleasure in cultivating a garden. In the fertile soil of her land, she sows seeds of abundance, nurturing plants that bear fruits and vegetables to nourish her loved ones. Through her labor and dedication, she provides not only sustenance but also a sense of connectedness to the natural world and the blessings it offers. (Proverbs 31:16, 24) Her pursuit of supporting and strengthening her household knows no bounds. She explores countless avenues, seizing opportunities that align with her values and goals. Whether it is through her craftsmanship, her artistic endeavors, or her wise investments, she seeks to enhance the financial stability and prosperity of her household.

7. Her heart overflows with boundless compassion, for she is not content to confine her care within the walls of her own household. Instead, she embraces the opportunity to extend a helping hand to those in need, demonstrating her deep empathy and selflessness. She remains aware of the needs of others, beyond her own husband and family, and grasps the larger picture of her family's place in the world. (Proverbs 31:20) With open arms and a listening ear, she becomes a beacon of hope for the downtrodden and the marginalized. She extends her kindness to the widows, the orphans, and the oppressed, recognizing their inherent worth and the value of their lives. She shares her resources, her time, and her wisdom, uplifting those burdened by life's hardships.

8. Mindful of her own self-care, she attends to her appearance and adorns herself beautifully. She takes intentional steps to maintain her physical health and appearance, understanding that her outward presentation can be a reflection of her inner character and self-respect. She engages in activities that promote vitality and strength, embracing a balanced lifestyle that encompasses proper nutrition, exercise, and self-care. (Proverbs 31:22)

9. Her husband, esteemed and respected, holds a position of honor in their community. His wisdom and trustworthiness are renowned within his sphere of influence. (Proverbs 31:23)

10. Displaying wisdom, she exercises control over her words, becoming an encourager and builder within her family and beyond. (Proverbs 31:25-26; Proverbs 14:1)

11. Her children look up to her as a role model, learning valuable life lessons through her words and deeds. They witness her unwavering love and dedication as she nurtures and guides them with wisdom and compassion. She instills in them the values of integrity, kindness, and perseverance, laying a strong foundation for their future. Her character and actions elicit honor and admiration from those closest to her. (Proverbs 31:28-30) Her husband, too, is in awe of her noble qualities. He sees her as his trusted companion and partner in life, appreciating her unwavering support, understanding, and unwavering love. He knows that she is a source of strength and encouragement, always by his side through thick and thin.

12. Having reaped numerous blessings and rewards, she should be able to revel in their fullness. A husband delights in his wife receiving recognition and praise, celebrating her achievements alongside her. (Proverbs 31:31)

13. She can hold positions of ministry within the church, as exemplified by the lives of notable women in the Kingdom of Yah. (Exodus 15:20, Judges 4:4, 2 Kings 22:14, Luke 2:36, Exodus 35:22-29, Philippians 4:3) The Most High God does not limit His calling based on gender but looks at the heart and the gifts bestowed upon individuals. Just as there were women in the ancient times who served Yah in significant roles, so can she.

In the Kingdom of Yah, there have been women of great faith and devotion who have played vital roles in spreading His Word and ministering to His people. Their lives serve as a testament to the limitless possibilities for women to serve in various capacities, guided by the Holy Spirit and empowered by their faith.

These women have stood as spiritual leaders, teachers, prophets, and evangelists, sharing the message of Yeshua and leading others on the path of righteousness. They have shown immense wisdom, compassion, and discernment, nurturing the spiritual growth of believers and bringing healing and restoration to those in need.

What About Submission?

Submission is often misconstrued and misused as a tool for manipulation and control. However, we must seek to understand YAH's true intention behind the concept of submission.

> **"Wives, submit yourselves unto your own husbands, as unto the Most High God."**
> **(Ephesians 5:22)**

Does this mean a wife becomes a servant or a slave, subjected to her husband's every whim? Certainly not. The husband, just like the wife, is called to be in submission to Yeshua's Word. In all of humanity, there is never a time when anyone is exempt from submission to someone else. The husband and wife form a partnership, working together as a team to advance YAH's Kingdom. They are designed to be interdependent, not independent. The female marriage partner, akin to a Vice-President, possesses her sphere of authority under her husband's direction. YAH has established an order of authority, and the husband bears the ultimate responsibility before YAH for all that occurs within his care. While it is a collaborative effort, someone must have the final say and shoulder the ultimate responsibility, and YAH has appointed the husband for this role. It is crucial for the wife to recognize and support her husband in this weighty responsibility.

The authority structure established by YAH follows the pattern of man, woman, and child, which echoes the fashion of elders. Thus, a woman is not considered equal to a man in terms of authority; rather, he has authority over her life without the dictatorship of an authoritarian. (Genesis 3:16, 1 Peter 3:1-6, Ephesians 5:19-33, 1 Corinthians 11:2-9)

Marriage should always be focused on the importance of an honorable wife and her qualities, rather than specifically addressing the duties or roles of a wife.

However, here are some additional points regarding the role of a wife in a marriage:

1. Love your husband unconditionally: Show love, appreciation, and affection to your husband both physically and emotionally. By offering unconditional love, you create a nurturing and supportive environment in your marriage.

2. Be a helper and support your husband: Stand by your husband and assist him in various aspects of life. Offer help and support during challenging times and work together as a team to achieve shared goals.

3. Maintain your husband's honor and dignity: Avoid speaking negatively about your husband to others and refrain from criticizing or belittling him in public. Resolve any issues or conflicts privately between the two of you.

4. Respect your husband: Value your husband's opinions, respect his decisions, and treat him with dignity. Communicate disagreements respectfully and constructively.

5. Fulfill your husband's needs: Understand and fulfill your husband's emotional, physical, and intimate needs. Create a nurturing and loving environment where both partners feel valued and cared for.

6. Seek your husband's opinion: Involve your husband in decision-making processes and value his input. Show that you respect and value his perspectives and ideas.

7. Take care of household duties: Contribute to the management of the household by keeping it organized, tidy, and clean. Involve other family members, including your husband and children, in sharing responsibilities.

8. Be responsible and prioritize self-care: Take responsibility for the well-being of your family, manage finances wisely, and take care of your own physical and emotional health. By prioritizing self-care, you can better care for your family.

It's important to note that the roles and responsibilities within a marriage can vary depending on cultural, societal, and individual factors. Open communication and mutual understanding between spouses are crucial in defining and fulfilling these roles in a way that suits the needs and dynamics of their relationship.

Does a wife have to obey her husband if she disagrees with his decision[s]?

As in any sacred covenant, let every effort be made to attain a virtuous agreement or concord. Yet, should such accord elude their grasp, then a Holy woman (fear of YAH) full of love submits to honor the commitment to follow her husband's decree, so long as it remains aligned with the divine precepts. However, if the decision transgresses the Word of YAH, the paramount allegiance to divine authority demands a respectful defiance. Let it be known that a wife shall never succumb to the temptation of treating her husband with disdain or scorn.

What happens if the wife is married to a profane man?

For the unbelieving husband is sanctified by the wife, and likewise, the unbelieving wife is sanctified by the husband; otherwise, your children would be deemed unclean, but now they are deemed holy. (1 Corinthians 7:14) Furthermore, dear wives, be in subjection to your own husbands, so that even if they disobey the Word, they may be won over without a word through the chaste and respectful conduct of their wives. (1 Peter 3:1)

Indeed, the non-believer husband must still be upheld in submission. It is not for wives to strive to convert their ungodly husbands through criticism, relentless evangelism, or coercing them into church attendance. The most powerful testimony lies in loving submission, akin to that shown to Christ, and a life guided by godliness. Only when a husband commits an offense that warrants divorce does the option of release become viable. Understand that no woman is compelled to be submissive to an abusive husband.

On a further note, the passage speaks to a specific woman's duty to be submissive to her particular husband, and not to every man. (Numbers 26:6)

What does a wife have the right to expect from her husband?

Let us have due reverence for the sacred bond, for the depths of the earth conceal abodes of cruelty. (Psalm 74:20) And behold, within this realm, there resides a man of YAH, renowned for his honor, and all that he proclaims surely comes to pass. Let us, therefore, approach him, perchance he may reveal the path we ought to tread. (1 Samuel 9:6) The woman spoke to Elijah, bearing witness, "Now I know that you are a man of YAH, and that the word of the Lord in your mouth is truth." (1 Kings 17:24) Hearken, my beloved brethren, has not YAH chosen those who are poor in the eyes of the world to be rich in faith and heirs of the kingdom? This is the promise to those who love Him. (James 2:5) May Christ dwell in your hearts through faith, as you are deeply rooted and grounded in love. (Ephesians 3:17) Let us approach with unwavering hearts, fully assured by faith, with our hearts sprinkled clean from an evil conscience and our bodies washed with pure water. (Hebrews 10:22) For I shall regard you with favor, making you fruitful and multiplying you, establishing my covenant with you. (Leviticus 26:9) O love the Lord, all you saints! The Lord preserves the faithful and rewards the doers of pride abundantly. (Psalm 31:23)

A trustworthy man of YAH possesses honor (Malachi 2:14, Ephesians 5:23), providing protection both financially and physically, as well as emotional sustenance (Ephesians 5:25). He holds a position of priority, forming an unbreakable union (Genesis 2:24, Matthew 19:5). Love graces their relationship (Colossians 3:19, Ephesians 5:25, 33), and the bond of intimacy finds its place (Genesis 2:25, Exodus 21:10, 1 Corinthians 7:2-4). Provision is given (Exodus 21:10), while consideration marks their interactions (1 Peter 3:7), and no belittling remarks are to be uttered (1 Peter 3:7, Deuteronomy 22:16-19). Cooperation is embraced (1 Peter 3:7).

Behind every prosperous man stands a woman. And if the man is united in marriage, then that woman surely is his wife. The role of a wife holds such significance that she has the power to either forge or shatter a family. She bestows upon her husband the strength to prevail, nurtures her children, safeguarding their well-being and future. With meticulous attention, she oversees the minutiae of the household.

So, what precisely does a wife undertake to hold such paramount importance within her family? Matrimony transforms a woman's life, as she transcends from a cherished, carefree maiden to a responsible wife, ready to embrace her marital duties. Let us examine these duties in detail:

Love him unconditionally: In the sacred bond of matrimony, a man yearns for affection, admiration, and love, just as a woman does. As a wife, bestow upon your husband unreserved love, both physically and emotionally. Shower him with appreciation, tending to his needs with the same tenderness as bestowed upon a child. In return, you shall receive his unconditional love.

Support him: Let no one claim that men are exempt from needing aid. We all seek support and solace. Become your husband's steadfast ally amidst adversity. Proactively extend your assistance whenever he seeks it. In turn, he shall reciprocate when you require his aid.

Uphold his honor and dignity: Refrain from speaking ill of your husband to your kin, friends, or acquaintances. Resist quarreling with him or uttering reproachful words in public. Forsake the temptations of gossip. Should any conflicts arise, resolve them in the sanctity of your union.

Stand by his side: A wife must stand beside her husband, embodying a unified front. Whether in daily endeavors or the pursuit of grand aspirations, offer unwavering support to your husband. Rejoice in being his companion on every step of his journey.

Be present for him: A husband yearns for the companionship of his wife, and likewise, a wife yearns for her husband's presence. Be readily available when he desires conversation. Listen attentively, offering guidance when necessary, and tend to his needs. Such actions epitomize your love and care.

Respect him: Show reverence for your husband. Value his opinions and hold him in high regard for who he is. In times of disagreement, voice your thoughts with gentleness, never allowing disrespect to permeate your words. Through your respect, you shall be met with respect.

Fulfill his needs: It may amuse or perturb you to witness your husband's reliance upon you, akin to that of a child. Do not be surprised if he cannot find what lies before his eyes and seeks your guidance. Do not question why he does not overtly express his appreciation for your presence. Instead, test his reliance by briefly withdrawing, and observe how deeply he longs for your return. A wife plays a pivotal role in fulfilling a man's needs.

Remain faithful: Upon entering the sacred bond of matrimony, you must exemplify loyalty and commitment to your husband, steadfastly, regardless of the circumstances. Let no shadow of doubt tarnish your faithfulness. Expect the same unwavering dedication from him.

Seek his counsel: Seeking your husband's opinion does not diminish your worth. Rather, it demonstrates your esteem for his judgment and respect for his wisdom.

Nourish him through culinary art: Pave the path to his heart by dishing out wholesome meals for your husband, just as you would for yourself. Resist the temptations of fast food along your daily journeys. Consider enlisting your husband's assistance in the kitchen, for it may serve as an opportunity to spend cherished time together.

Respect your in-laws: Regardless of cultural or lifestyle differences, hold respect for your husband's parents, for they are an intrinsic part of his life. In doing so, you inspire your husband to reciprocate the same reverence toward your parents.

Attend to household duties: Maintain a well-ordered and immaculate household. Seek aid from your husband and children, assigning them tasks to foster a sense of responsibility within the family unit.

Shoulder your responsibilities: Being a responsible wife is a boon to the family, for it engenders a sense of direction and purpose. Undertake the management of the household, finances, and the upbringing of your children with utmost diligence.

Exercise patience: Patience is a virtue that does not come effortlessly. When juggling multiple responsibilities daily, and the path veers from your intended course, patience tends to be the last thing on your mind. However, strive to cultivate patience within yourself, and you shall not be disappointed. Picture a scenario where you find yourself in a rush to depart for work, and your husband engages you in seemingly trivial matters. Suppress your haste, for he may simply be seeking playful banter. Had you embraced patience that morning, your day would have unfolded more favorably for both you and your husband.

Educate your children: Parenting is a shared responsibility between a mother and a father. Yet, a mother plays an instrumental role in the education of her children, possessing an intimate understanding of their innermost selves and endowed with the patience and time to devote to their growth.

Preserve the sanctity of your home: Safeguard your abode from intruders, both physical and those who seek to inject venomous thoughts into the minds of your loved ones. Distance yourself from individuals steeped in negativity.

Care for yourself: Nay, it is not the final task to tend to. In truth, you ought to prioritize your own well-being before tending to others, for the happiness and vitality of your family hinge upon your own. Do not burden yourself with overwhelming responsibilities. Seek assistance from your kin, embrace moments of respite and tranquility. Thus shall you preserve your radiant smile, and the countenance of a joyful wife shall be a sight most pleasing to behold by your husband.

In adhering to these duties, a wife brings harmony, stability, and joy to her family. Her dedication knows no bounds, for she embraces the profound meaning behind each word she utters and every action she undertakes. In the depths of her devotion, the sanctity of marriage flourishes, and her family thrives.

The Honor a Wife Upholds in Marriage:

1. Be a helper to your husband.

While all individuals are called to be helpers to others, the Word places a special emphasis on this responsibility for wives. Genesis tells us that Yah realized it wasn't good for man to be alone, and that He decided to make a "helper suitable for him" (Gen. 2:18). It is interesting to note that the Hebrew meaning of the word helper in this passage is found hereafter in the Word to refer only to Yah as He helps us. The fact that this same word is applied to a wife signifies that women have been given tremendous power for good in their husbands' lives. Yah has designed wives to help their husbands become all that Yah intends for them to be.

2. Respect your husband.

In Ephesians 5:33, Paul says, "... the wife must respect her husband." When you respect your husband, you reverence him, notice him, regard him, honor him, prefer him, and esteem him. It means valuing his opinion, admiring his wisdom and character, appreciating his commitment to you, and considering his needs and values.

Husbands have many needs to be fulfilled in a relationship. A man does well to openly communicate by providing a list of primary needs most men have to his wife.

Self-confidence in his manhood: To be listened to, Companionship, To be needed

Meeting these needs is what respecting your husband is all about. An example would be a wife who becomes her husband's number one fan is a boost to morale and self-confidence. Every husband wants his wife to be on his team, to coach him when necessary, but most of all to be his cheerleader. A husband needs a wife who is behind him, believing in him, appreciating him, and cheering him on as he goes out into the world every day.

3. Love your husband.

Titus 2:4 calls for wives "to love their husbands." A good description of the kind of love your husband needs is "unconditional acceptance." In other words, accept your husband just as he is—an imperfect person. Love also means being committed to a mutually fulfilling sexual relationship. I realize there is a whole lot more to love than sex, but we are looking at how to fulfill Yah's command to love our husbands. Therefore, we must look at love from their perspective, not just our own.

Surveys show that sex is one of a man's most important needs—if not the most important. When a wife resists intimacy, is uninterested, or is only passively interested, her husband may feel rejection. It will cut at his self-image, tear at him to the very center of his being, and create isolation.

Taking pride of her husband, a woman walks in honor of love to ensure her husband's well-being is not neglected for a happy life. She takes a look at her relationship and says:

My husband's sexual needs should be more important and higher on my priority list than menus, housework, projects, activities, and even the children. It does not mean that I should think about sex all day and every day, but it does mean that I find ways to remember my husband and his needs. It means I save some of my energy for him. This keeps me from being selfish and living only for my own needs and wants. Maintaining that focus helps me defeat isolation in our marriage.

4. Submit to the leadership of your husband.

Just mention the word "submission," and many women immediately become angry and even hostile. Some husbands and wives actually believe submission infers that women are inferior to men in some way. Some women think that if they submit, they will lose their identity and become non-persons. Others fear (some with good reason) that submission leads to being used or abused.

Another misconception is that submission means blind obedience on the part of the woman. She can give no input to her husband, question nothing, and only stay obediently barefoot and pregnant in the kitchen.

What does Yah have in mind? Here's a key passage from the Word:

Wives, be subject to your own husbands, as to Yah. For the husband is the head of the wife, as Christ also is the head of the church, Christ being the Savior of the body. Just as the church is subject to Christ, so also the wives ought to be to their husbands in everything. Husbands, love your wives, just as Christ also loved the church and gave Himself up for her, so that He might sanctify her, having cleansed her by the washing of water with the word, that He might present to Himself the church in all her glory, having no spot or wrinkle or any such thing; but that she would be holy and blameless. So, husbands ought also to love their own wives as their own bodies. He who loves his own wife loves himself; for no one ever hated his own flesh, but nourishes and cherishes it, just as Christ also does the church, because we are members of His body. —Ephesians 5:22-30

Yah's plan for marriage involves mutual love, respect, and partnership between spouses. It does not condone or endorse abusive or harmful behavior. While submission is encouraged, it should be within the context of a loving and respectful relationship. If a husband's actions or behaviors are significantly destructive or harmful, it is essential to seek help, establish healthy boundaries, and prioritize the well-being and safety of yourself and your children.

Aiding my husband in fulfilling Yah's divine purpose for his life

These Scriptures make it clear that a wife should submit voluntarily to her husband's sensitive and loving leadership. Therefore, as I voluntarily submit to my husband, I am completing him. I am helping him fulfill his responsibilities, and I am helping him become the man, the husband, and the leader Yah intended him to be.

Building oneness in marriage works best when both spouses choose to fulfill their responsibilities voluntarily, with no pressure or coercion. A woman in submission to graciously respect her husband allows him to fulfill the role as a servant-leader. This allows the husband to love his wife as he is commanded.

I do this with an attitude of entrusting myself to Yah. In one of his letters, Peter told us that even though Yeshua suffered terrible pain and insults, He did not retaliate "but kept entrusting Himself to Him who judges righteously" (1 Peter 2:23). When you entrust your life to the Father, it's much easier to be the wife of an imperfect man, particularly when you may have disagreements.

A special note: Some of you may live with abuse or in excessively unhealthy and destructive conditions in your marriage. At times, it may be inappropriate or even life-threatening for you to apply unquestioningly the principles of submission. For example, if you are being physically or verbally abused, you need to take steps to protect yourself and your children. Should you find yourself in such a circumstance, it's advisable to carefully seek guidance from counselors with training or trustworthy elders who possess marital experience and wisdom. Their insights can be valuable in addressing your particular concerns. Please recognize that the roles within a respectful marriage hold a sacred significance of honor and glory, as their virtue is rooted in principles of sanctity. However, it is crucial to seek wisdom, discernment, and guidance, especially in situations involving abuse or excessively unhealthy and destructive conditions within a marriage. In such cases, prioritizing personal safety and seeking professional help is necessary.

Loving, forgiving, and submitting in a marriage does not mean that you should become a passive doormat or tolerate destructive behavior indefinitely. As we acknowledge Yah as the Most High God and Lord of our lives, we must work out our marriages according to His plan. It is important for each wife to follow Yah's plan, understand her role, and work in harmony with her husband's responsibilities.[1]

Remember, Yah's plan for marriage is based on love, grace, and the well-being of both partners. It is important to seek guidance, counsel, and support from wise and trusted individuals of good moral standard, such as pastors, counselors, or married couples over 20 years who can help navigate challenging situations and ensure that your marriage aligns with YAH's principles of love, respect, and mutual well-being.

The ultimate reward for honoring the authority of Almighty YAH is the transition from mortal life to immortality. It is with love, faith, and charity, embracing humility within the established authority ordained by Almighty YAH, that we should eagerly strive toward the kingdom, knowing that the fear of the Most High God brings the presence of eternal life. (1 Corinthians 15:53-54, 1 Timothy 1:16-17, 6:10-16, Romans 2:1-7)

Let us, therefore, move swiftly and resolutely toward the kingdom, guided by love, faith, and charity, as we embrace the authority established by the Almighty YAH, knowing that it leads to eternal life in His presence.

---

[1]   Glenn Davis. (2004-2022) The Biblical Role Of The Wife https://www.free-bible-study-lessons.com/wife.html Accessed 2021

The Sacred Duty of Maternal Role

One of the most significant roles that a mother assumeth is the role of a nurturer. This term is oftentimes used interchangeably with the term "mother." When a mother doth nurture her children well, love and virtue are awakened within the depths of their tender hearts. Through the love bestowed by our mothers, we doth learn to love in return, and we doth experience the profound love of Yah.

This role encompasseth all forms of motherhood. There is no perfect path to motherhood, for mothers find themselves in diverse circumstances. Some may lack husbands, while others dwell with female partners. Some conform to conventional family structures, whilst others rear their children with the aid of the "village." Some are stay-at-home mothers, whilst others toil in the workforce. Each mother hath her own unique set of skills and challenges, and her children, too, are of varied nature. All such situations are valid, for what truly mattereth is that a mother loveth her children with utmost devotion. The role of a mother is to pour forth love from the depths of her being.

Traditionally, within the family unit, the mother's role hath been to raise the children and attend to household tasks. Yet, the role of mothers within the home is ever evolving. Mothers are increasingly shouldering multiple responsibilities, such as engaging in work whilst caring for the young ones simultaneously.

As mothers bring forth life into this world, it is only fitting that they remain at home and form a bond with the newborn, particularly during the initial stages. The wisdom and knowledge that a mother doth impart unto her children aideth them in blossoming into virtuous young adults. For single mothers, the burden is even greater, as they bear the sole weight of parenting without a partner or husband.

Furthermore, it is the duty of every mother to comprehend her children. When a child perceiveth this, he or she doth learn to place trust in the parent(s) more deeply. Active listening is paramount to understanding. Thus, it is of utmost importance for mothers to truly listen to their children. Shama, a Hebrew word signifying "to hear intelligently," must be exercised by mothers to understand, support, and love their children.

Indeed, one of the most profound roles that a mother fulfills is that of a nurturer. This term is oftentimes employed as a synonym for "mother." When a mother doth nurture her children with care, love and righteousness are kindled within the depths of their tender hearts. Through the love bestowed by our mothers, we doth learn to love in return, and we doth experience the profound love of Yah.

Many among us are familiar with the African proverb, "It takes a village to raise a child." It holds true that numerous individuals influence the development of a child as they journey toward adulthood: family members, friends, teachers, and others. However, many of us would concur that certain influential figures assume center stage in a child's life during crucial stages of development, aiding them in becoming virtuous, capable, resilient, and moral individuals. One of these paramount influencers beareth the revered title of "Mother."

Teaching children within the confines of the home is of paramount importance, particularly given the moral climate we find ourselves amidst in this present age. Parents must firmly resolve that teaching within the home is a primary duty and endeavor to raise children who are well-adjusted, confident, and content. While other social institutions, such as the church and school, may lend aid in "training up a child in the way he should go" (Proverbs 22:6), the ultimate responsibility resteth with the parents. According to the divine plan of Yah, it is unto parents that He entrusteth the care and nurturing of His beloved children.

A Mother is entrusted by Yah to labor alongside the Father in the upbringing of their children and the safeguarding of every soul entrusted unto their care. Recognizing this truth is to comprehend the vital role that mothers play in the lives of their offspring. They wield great influence over them, and thus it behooves mothers to exercise wisdom and righteousness throughout the span of their days—a task that may oftentimes appear formidable. However, motherhood is accompanied by this weighty responsibility.

Indeed, these are among the roles fulfilled by our mothers. Yet, what about our own roles? Our mothers deserve boundless love for the risks they undertake during childbirth, for raising us amidst times of adversity, and for ceaselessly guiding and loving us. In response, let us extend our gratitude, respect, and trust unto them. Let us listen attentively to their counsel and consistently lend them our assistance in whatever manner we are able.

"A mother's nurturing love awakens in children, from their earliest moments upon this earthly plane, a remembrance of the love and goodness they experienced in their pre-mortal existence," declares one wise teacher. "Through the love bestowed upon us by our mothers, we learn—or rather, we remember—that YAH also loves us."

Other prophets and apostles further teach that the work of nurturing holds eternal significance, and it can be exercised throughout one's life, whether or not a woman has children of her own. If you are a mother, you partake in Yah's creative work—not solely by granting physical bodies to your offspring but also by instructing and nurturing them. And if you are not a mother at present, the creative talents you cultivate shall prepare you for that eventual day, be it in this life or the next.

"Who can truly measure the righteous influence of a mother's love? What enduring fruits arise from the seeds of truth that a mother diligently plants and tenderly nurtures within the fertile soil of a child's trusting mind and heart?"

"As a mother, you have been endowed with divine instincts that aid you in perceiving your child's unique talents and individual capacities."

Let us, therefore, learn from our own mothers the lessons of courage, strength, and hope. They possess a sacred role not only in our lives but also in our society and in the world at large.

Both parents ought to embrace the responsibility of instructing their children. However, by divine design, motherhood places a particular emphasis on nurturing and teaching the next generation. As the vices prevalent in society grow increasingly pervasive, the presence and influence of a loving mother who imparts correct principles to her children within the home serve as an additional layer of protection, shielding them from harmful and destructive worldly influences.

1. A Mother as the Primary Educator

A mother assumes the pivotal role of being the first teacher to her child. Bestowed with the precious gift of a child by Yah, parents bear the responsibility of nurturing and guiding their offspring. This noble duty requires immense patience and unwavering dedication. As children possess remarkably impressionable minds, they observe and emulate nearly everything they witness. While the responsibility of raising happy and positive children falls upon both parents, it is often the mother who spends the majority of the day with the child, fulfilling needs that only a mother can fulfill. Thus, due to the extensive time a mother spends with her baby, she becomes the child's first teacher, and the child trusts and follows her guidance wholeheartedly.

2. A Mother as a Nurturer

With no intention to diminish the significance of fathers, it is acknowledged that mothers hold a slightly greater influence in a child's nurturing. Mothers possess an instinctive ability to be attuned to their children, reading their cues right from the moment of birth. An indescribable emotional connection exists between a mother and her child, one that cannot be replicated by a father alone. As mothers, it is crucial to remain observant and discern any emotional, physical, or behavioral changes in our children. By doing so, we can identify and address any issues at their earliest stages, preventing them from escalating into more significant problems.

3. A Mother as a Secure Anchor

Merely days after birth, a baby begins recognizing the scent and face of their mother. From that point forward, a mother's presence, touch, and voice become a secure foundation for the child. The phrase "I want my mommy" often arises as the immediate response to any distress encountered by the child. Therefore, it is paramount for mothers to nurture and fortify this unwavering bond between themselves and their children. It is essential to avoid unreasonable anger, impatience, spanking, or public shaming, as such actions can swiftly erode the trust built with the child. As the first teacher, a mother must create an environment in which her child feels safe and secure. While this role may be taken for granted at times, its significance should never be underestimated, as insecurity can contribute to various emotional and psychological challenges faced by the child.

4. A Mother as a Confidant

A mother possesses the remarkable ability to comprehend her children not only through their expressions and body language but also through open conversations about their experiences and emotions. Women tend to be more verbal than men, and mothers, being better listeners, create an environment where children find it easier to confide in them when they are troubled. Even in the absence of problems, mothers consistently display genuine interest in their children's lives, asking thoughtful questions and adeptly eliciting responses. As a mother, it is crucial to maintain open and active communication with our children throughout their journey into adulthood. As children grow older, they may begin to confide more in their friends than their parents. To counter this, we should strive to be their friends, engaging in daily interactions and sharing laughter, rather than solely entering conversations when troubles arise. As the first teacher, a mother imparts knowledge and spends ample time with her child, fostering a deep connection.

5. A Mother as an Emotional Anchor

While women and their emotions are occasionally the subject of jests, it is through their emotional capacity that mothers form profound connections with their children. Mothers are unhesitant to offer hugs or shed tears alongside their children in public, a practice fathers may shy away from. Mothers possess the ability to discuss emotions with their children, helping them develop better emotional resilience. They possess an innate understanding of their child's needs and moods, even when their child's words are limited. This emotional security is paramount in a child's development. Combined with their role as nurturers, mothers have the power to enhance their child's emotional intelligence and sensitivity towards others. Thus, a mother serves as the first teacher in a child's life, imparting invaluable lessons.

6. A Mother as an Educator

Mothers naturally serve as the original pre-school for their children. They are more likely to engage their children in various learning activities, from singing rhymes aloud to solving puzzles, as they excel in communication. Moreover, mothers possess a playful demeanor and demonstrate remarkable patience in accommodating their child's learning pace. They are adept at teaching children soft skills. As a mother, it is vital to interact with your child as much as possible, assisting them in their initial learning stages and helping them develop organizational skills as they gain independence. Being the first teacher, a mother spends substantial time with her child, fulfilling the role of an educator.

7. A Mother as a Disciplinarian

A mother must strike a balance between being strict and offering affectionate care to her child. It is her responsibility to instill a sense of responsibility within the child, teaching them their first life lessons. A mother aids her child in understanding verbal instructions and enables them to express their needs. She plays a pivotal role in toilet training and mentally preparing her child to face the outside world when they embark on their first school experience.

Creating an Environment of Positive Teaching and Parent-Child Interaction:

To foster an environment of positive and uplifting teaching within the home, where parents and children can spend quality time together, consider the following ideas:

1. Family Night: Dedicate one night each week exclusively to your family. Utilize this time for bonding, engaging in activities that bring joy, reading scriptures, and discussing matters of importance. Make an effort to create lasting memories.

2. Shared Meals: Studies demonstrate that shared family meals strengthen the bonds between family members, promote well-adjusted children, and reduce obesity. Utilize meal times to inquire about each other's daily activities, providing support and encouragement.

3. Family Prayer: Gather your children each evening for a family prayer. Express gratitude for the blessings bestowed upon each family member individually and collectively, and humbly ask for guidance and provision.

By embracing these practices, a mother can fulfill her role as the first teacher and create an atmosphere where children thrive.

To show gratitude to their mothers, fathers can:

1. Show appreciation: Express gratitude and validate the efforts of their wives every day. Notice and acknowledge the work she does and say thank you frequently.

2. Spend quality time together: Schedule evenings or dedicated time for just the two of them to connect and strengthen their bond.

3. Share parenting responsibilities: Have regular conversations with their wives about each child's needs and discuss ways they can contribute and help with parenting duties.

4. Give their wives breaks: Offer their wives a "day away" now and then, where they take over the household responsibilities and allow their wives to have a break from their daily routine.

5. Be present and engaged: When fathers come home from work, they should actively participate in family life. Prioritize listening to, playing with, and teaching their children, without putting work, friends, or hobbies ahead of family time.

Children can show gratitude to their mothers by:

1. Taking responsibility: Clean up after themselves by picking up toys when they're finished playing with them. As they get older, they can also contribute by making their bed, helping with the dishes, and doing other chores without being asked.[2]

2. Saying thank you: Express gratitude more often for things their mothers do, such as preparing a nice meal, reading them a bedtime story, or taking care of their clothes.

3. Showing affection: Hug their mothers often and express their love for them through words and actions.

By implementing these gestures of gratitude, both fathers and children can demonstrate their appreciation and strengthen the bond with their mothers.

---

[2] Waterford.org. (2021) How to Help Your Children Grow an Attitude of Gratitude. https://www.waterford.org/resources/help-your-children-grow-gratitude/ Accessed 2021

The Dutiful Gentleman

Who among men is prepared to shoulder the weight of a woman? A man who comprehends his responsibilities, therefore, shall avert great devastation. Doth the woman share like aspirations to fulfill thy destiny? Doth harmony and reverence thrive after discord? A man who proposes to unite with a woman, not swayed by mere infatuation, but by sound reasons and resolute commitment, perchance may find success.

Before the union of man and woman transpires, prudent it is to seek counsel for the unforeseen. Let a man's heart be steadfast as a rock, built upon unwavering values, fortified by the passage of time, and cognizant of his interactions with others before the foundation of a home be laid.

Naught shall sunder this foundation as he invests faithfully in those who dwell within. If a man chooses sagaciously, he shall first establish honor and discipline as a way of life, mutually agreeable. Secondly, he shall establish the order of provision for common necessities and security. A man's character is revealed through his deeds, betraying the essence of his heart. Though some may surmise, the thoughts of a man remain concealed, shared solely with those closest. The maturity of a man mirrors the seasons of trees, planted in due time, testing the mettle of their endurance. Only through conquering obstacles with consideration for others shall a man prove his worth. A man who aspires to lead others must forsake selfish desires, forsaking personal interests and turning a blind eye to the injustices befalling others. Forsooth, should he fail to do so, those who follow may be ensnared in a distorted reality, entangled in fragmented concerns. As trees are felled by the striking hand, so may some souls vanish beyond reclamation. Others may slumber, bereft of concern, steadfastly adhering to the status quo.

The Man

What man is ready to take on the responsibility of a woman? A man who does not know his roles could greatly devastate the occasion. Does the woman have the same goals in mind to fulfill your destiny? Is there a happy balance of respect for cooperation after disagreement? A man who proposes to unite with a woman for sound reasons to fulfill his responsibility beyond puppy love has a chance.

Prior to any union of a man and woman taking place, it is wise to consider to have counsel for the unforeseen. A man's heart must be like a rock of stable values that get only better with time as he is conscious and fully aware of his interactions with others before the building foundation of a home.

Nothing can destroy it as he faithfully invests in those within it. If a man chooses wisely, he establishes first the honor and discipline for a way of life mutually agreeable and, secondly, the order of provision for common necessity and security. A man is known by his actions as to what heart lies within. The thoughts of a man who can tell save those closest even if they have somewhat of a clue. The maturity of a man is like the nature of trees planted in their seasons of life that take a course to prove whether their durability will endure throughout time. The only difference is overcoming obstacles faced in consideration of others. A man planning to lead others must be selfless, not absorbed in personal interest, only that the injustice of others is overlooked. Otherwise, those following may be subject to the distortion of being concerned in matters not viewed as a whole. Consequently, as trees are struck, so shall some fall away, never to return? Some may remain asleep, having no concerns as they are persistent in following the status quo.

There are those who inquire to raise concerns to higher standards, having patience to endure as an ultimatum establishes the release or determination of compromise to remain. Lastly, due to the lack of concern, some may result to go and come as they please not fully committed to the leadership provided thus weakening the relationship.

Man is the defender, protector, and leader of the family as he carefully plans to make decisions with his family for the sake unity. A leader must be strong not rude, kind not weak, bold without oppression, thoughtful not arrogant, and humble to grow around others for the inspiration of hope. A man's intelligence does not submit to ignorance. Ignorance rejects something one knows nothing about. A man not subject to discipline or has ego may not follow instructions well.

A great amount of effort to be open for correction are the humble beginnings to maintain quality lifestyle. A man develops his character of ethics by craft, trade, or any other activity that asserts will power over one's base desires for self-control. The motivation that a man has is self-discipline. Self-discipline is the reason of determination that a man chooses the best course of action in pursuit of his desire. Time management is an important skill of decision making for self-control; as it determines the quality of life one chooses.

The young man who inquires for truth within himself, finding his place within the universe; may find that he is capable to take on such a role of leadership even marriage. Without the mastery of craft, a man's provision may not yield substantially for the support of others. Neither will he have the time to inspire a child's new gift. Having little insight neither the experience in preparation of a home's foundation; a man's authority is limited to his craft as it dictates his availability throughout the hours of the day. The situation does not socially and economically warrant a man to become lord of his home as he is subject to the craft of hire. Howbeit, the man is the provider and protector of the home that a woman may extend the provision of charity to glorify it. A poor man does not have a place to hang out. Only by observing universal laws does he gain wisdom of his surroundings to have authority over the life he encounters. If the woman does not respect what a man does, she will not support him. A man cannot forget his friends to be absorbed in someone else's world.

In other cases, where a man is not the sole provider financially, let his contribution be received without penalty. No matter the salary, let a woman not flex her muscle to subdue him in success. Better is it to share a fortune than to grow old in depreciation of lonely ego for status.

A grateful relationship is equally balanced by what both have to offer as one is to complement the other so that there is no imbalance. Wisdom is the divine intervention that a man must use determine what is best in the case he is not the sole provider to offset the imbalance of support. The work a union creates is harmony which is not always easy as roles are not always traditional, but a work of progress continues to play till the right tune compliments the other.

The common thread of communication shared to establish principal grounds of honor for a committed trusting relationship ensures no confusion for entertainment by speculation or curiosity. The perception of one's imagination can run wild as a fire of insecurities that may discomfort to disrupt the soul of peace. A wise man, who desires to lead, rarely risks anything in ignorance to suffer the consequence.

A man whose mother transcends his authority for the request of many demands becomes a servant at will. The instances of insults that is likely to occur, verbally abuses and ruin the heart of a man. If a love-hate relationship develops, a dysfunction for a lack of compassion and consideration towards women may be present alongside the prevention of a mature love. Letting others raise a son does not instill a stable relationship of a man's love for a woman. A love-hate relationship is just enough to keep a man in bondage. Love alone is not enough to keep a home. An unstable man is dependent upon whatever resources are necessary to make ends meet for survival.

A man lacking compassion is blinded by the selfishness of his own heart. Difficult is it to consider another's wellbeing to behold what countenance is present so that humanity be not devalued. The only evil that exists is within the nature of one's thoughts. A man's thoughts open doors for all manner of activity whether good or evil; one should not blame society for circumstances. Rather, choose wisely the path to good fortune than to complain without self-accountability to cover up the mess of shame. Whatever shame not rectified of the present, yet incurred of the past shall the disgust be uncovered by another. Commonly, the quitter of any relationship is often a habitual offender resisting change for the sake of preserving humanity which gives life to the air we breathe.

A compassionate heart seeks meekly through observation to become knowledgeable, can by wisdom unlock the heart of neglected situations experienced by the fatherless, widow, orphan, and even the stranger. Walking in the shoes of others is the experience that recognizes signs of distress that most suffer. Anyone can become blind not to consider one's ways to choose wisely a relationship without the hassle of pain. A man who leads wisely remains inclusive of others without threat or force to dominate any view of opposition by persuasion.

A father is to give instruction in righteousness that the house stands in honor of justice and equality without partiality. Ruling in the favor of love, a father takes charge over his family to ensure the peace of longevity. The questioning and provoking of his authority for reasoning with suspicion is an unpleasant taste of disgust not to be discussed. Disrespect is the bitterness and rottenness of his bones as he seeks the peace of his home. The rod shall not be spared for any iniquity of crookedness as he makes his paths strait to walk honorably with an upright heart. All that is of his possession shall find it wise to seek peace than to challenge him disrespectfully.

Rarely is there a factor of outside influence to interfere with his governing of courtship as he is entrusted head of estate. The daughter is not to leave her Father's authority till the day of his consent is transferred to her beloved by promise and blessing; knowing that she has not power over her own body to do so what she pleases for the honor of her Father remains as the extension of his family. The father determines whether a man is capable of leading, listening, and having an understanding heart to address concerns, desires, and issues necessary to comfort her.

The son is groomed from the years of adolescence till he matures sound in discipline, craft, and keen judgment. Hopefully the mother has weaned her son from dependency to relinquish her authority and to bestow a new respect for him as a man of authority for government. Once a father recognizes his son's craft is mastered in stability teaching him the difficulties of life as a provider and leader of the house, a son equipped to lead his home.

A husband must prepare is heart to deal with the issues of life that takes on burdens to protect the family. Having an understanding heart, the man cannot be rash causing the wife and children to grieve. A husband entrusted with the lives of his courtship must continue to be a seeker of knowledge to instruct the family in righteousness of his domain. Therefore, let him choose a wife of encouragement willing to support the establishment of his courtship. In honor and dignity, a woman possesses the freedom she desires to fulfill her needs to nourish the home.

A husband is very much delighted to have the support of his wife freely as it displeases him sorely otherwise. The wife's support brings such an energy of attraction that a man finds it priceless to compare; being compelled by the feeling he fulfills what is most precious to him. A woman that desires to make herself ready (surrender for sake of peace) for her beloved husband is the most precious gift on earth he can receive.

The less one fights the more can be accomplished in unison. Much patience is required of a man that in due time knowledge of the desires of her heart may yield the treasures of life continually for a legacy.

A man becomes a brother to those he offers his home, whether it be in times of need or as a gift of love. He respects others equally without pride or lifting his voice over them. The authority of command is respected and shared equally, without abuse to dictate the lead of other men astray from a natural relationship of peace where every man is commonly at ease. A man listens carefully and quickly to another not for self-esteem but to know his brother as himself. This important skill is necessary for a common thread of unity to exist between the courtships of families that honor peace kept sacred throughout the land. A selfless man cares for the lives of others than to take away the substance of life without promise. It is better to give than to receive that good fortune comes not by greed.

The Husband and Yah's Divine Order

Yah has designed the world around a system of authority. Everyone is under someone's authority. Ultimately, all authority is delegated authority under Yah. The person who exercises authority [or refuses to do so] is responsible to Yah. Misuse of authority in any sphere - government, family, church, etc. - leads to the judgment of Yah for misrepresenting His character.

The authority structure, as it relates to the family, places the husband and wife as a team much like the President and the Vice President. They should work together to build a life and the Kingdom of Yah by solving problems in a more holistic way. However, in cases where agreement cannot be reached, someone must have the authority to make the final decision. Yah has placed that authority in the husband.

Many times, we sinfully stop at the first phrase. We stress that the husband is the head of the wife while ignoring the rest of the sentence. The husband is to be the head of the wife in the same way that Yeshua is the head of the Church and is its Savior.

How is Yeshua the head of the Church? He is the Leader of the Church, but all His decisions are made for the benefit of the Church. He makes NO decisions from selfish motives. Sometimes He makes hard decisions, but always for the ultimate benefit of the Church. In fact, His love for the Church went so far as the giving up of His body to torture and death for her.

In the same way, the husband may need to make tough decisions, but they are to always be for the benefit of his wife and children. He is to always place their needs and desires above his own. As a human being, the husband deals with his own sinful nature and needs the counsel of his wife on reaching the best decisions. Yah placed them together as a team. However, when the time for a decision comes, he is the one who stands responsible before Yah for making it... and for its consequences. It is a heavy responsibility, not a power trip.

The husband is the savior of his wife the same way that Yeshua is the Savior of the church. Just as Yeshua can restore forgiveness of sin so can the husband forgive his wife to make her whole for they are one flesh. (Eph 5:24-27, Matt 23:10, Gen 2:24, 3:16) The husband's duty is to lead his wife by a standard established in the ways of Yah. He studies the Word of Yah to reveal the manifestation of his faith. A man of peace prospers having a testimony of overcoming all odds against life and peace (spiritual journey) to lead in the ways of righteousness. And just as Yeshua gave His life for the Church, the husband must be willing to sacrifice his physical life if necessary to save the life of his wife. Part of this also includes, as we have written elsewhere, making sure his wife is properly cared for should he die before she does. It should be obvious from the above that the husband is not an independent authority. He only has legitimate authority as he is submitted to the authority of Yeshua. He does not make decisions or take actions based on his own feelings, desires, or wisdom. He must study and know the Word of Yah, be submitted to it, and apply it in love.

So, husbands, you are the managers under Yah of your home. You are responsible before Yah for everything that goes on in it. If there isn't enough love [or anything else] in the home, don't complain, don't blame your wife. It's your fault...and your responsibility to take charge and fix it with virtuous solutions. [This is a blunt statement meant to remove excuses and blame shifting. I know where there are problems usually both parties bear some blame and must work together to find solutions. I also know that in some cases a wife has been so hurt by her husband or by incidents in her past or simply the desire to engage our sinful nature that nothing the husband does will restore the relationship. A husband is to do his best with the love of Yeshua to minister to his wife, but he does not walk in guilt and condemnation. So, while I place strong responsibility on the husband, in cases like those mentioned above, it may not be his fault. There may be nothing he can do to fix it.]

Husbands, you cannot do this on your own. It will break you. You need the power of the Holy Spirit...and you need an assistant. Yah, in His wisdom, provided you with a lovely and competent assistant.

"And the Almighty Yah caused a deep sleep to fall upon Adam, and he slept: and he took one of his ribs, and closed up the flesh instead thereof; And the rib, which the Almighty Yah had taken from man, made he a woman, and brought her unto the man. And Adam said, This is now bone of my bones, and flesh of my flesh: she shall be called Woman, because she was taken out of Man." Gen. 2:21-23

> **"For the husband is the head of the wife, even as Yeshua is the head of the church: and he is the savior of the body." Eph. 5:23**

The Priority Relationship

This is one reason why the husband/wife relationship is the most important human relationship. It is more important than the parent/child relationship. It is more important than the husband's or wife's relationship with their own parents. Certainly, it is vastly more important than relationships with friends outside the home. The husband/wife relationship is the priority relationship. Only our relationship with Yah is more important.

"Therefore shall a man leave his father and his mother, and shall cleave unto his wife: and they shall be one flesh." Gen. 2:24

The husband is to take time to understand and minister to his wife. This is especially important in the first year of marriage when so much change and adjustment is taking place [Deut. 24:5, Col. 3:19]. Take time out from the business of life to enjoy your wife. Dating does not stop when you get married! Continue to have fun together [Ecc. 9:9]. In line with this, the husband is to be an encourager. It is so tempting to criticize, complain, and make hurting comments. That is not how Yeshua treats His Church. He treasures it as a husband is commanded to love so must his heart treasure his wife.

He welcomes every opportunity to build her up and encourage her. He seeks to be her biggest promoter upholding her image with pride praising her success in any area of life.

> **"Her children arise up, and call her blessed; her husband also, and he praiseth her." Pr. 31:28**

Another role of the husband is to be his wife's lover. A husband should meet his wife's sexual needs. Sex is to be an act of giving; it is being more concerned about fulfilling the needs of the wife than receiving fulfillment. The husband must understand that his wife views sex differently and different things minister to her needs. He must be gentle and kind. He must not be too proud to ask his wife what meets her desires. Researching with doers of the word, tasteful but detailed books [like Act of Marriage or Intended for Pleasure] is recommended. Note: Trying to use X-rated movies or other pornographic material to improve the sexual relationship is lustful and extremely harmful to the relationship.

"And they were both naked, the man and his wife, and were not ashamed." Gen. 2:25

"The wife hath not power of her own body, but the husband: and likewise also the husband hath not power of his own body, but the wife." 1 Cor. 7:4

Life ought not be filled with condemnation, but challenges us to seek out eternal life. If our relationship is less than it should be, let us take on the responsibility to find solutions that maintain love of peace and joy. We may need to humbly seek the forgiveness of our wife for having failed her. Husbands known as Servant Leaders are humble people. Therefore we prove the sincerity of our repentance by changing to become Holy (fear of YAH) husbands. May Yah help us for with Him all things are possible, but without Him failure is inevitable.

What if a man's wife does not follow his leadership? Should he try to force her to submit? How does Yeshua deal with His Church when it doesn't submit to Him? Yeshua continues to lead. He does not compromise Holy principles to gain cooperation. He continues to love and provide for His Church. His love is shown in His faithfulness and care even when His Church does not deserve it. He does not use violence or manipulation to attempt to force or trick His Church into obedience. Certainly, it is a difficult position to be in, but study the actions of Yeshua with His Church for the principles of how to operate.

Most wives will not have a problem with submission if they know their husbands are genuinely following Yah and doing their best for their wives and families. Divorce becomes a viable choice only when the wife is proven guilty of persistent sinful behavior that constitutes grounds for ending the marriage. No husband is required to remain married to a woman who deliberately pursues a sinful lifestyle.

Finally, is the role of the husband different for Christians and non-believers? No, Yah's standards in every area of life are the same for His entire human creation. As sinful creatures we will always fall below the perfect standard set by Yeshua; however, empowered by the Holy Spirit, it should be our goal. We should never be satisfied with less than the best. Among Israelite and Christian men (believers of YAH), it's unfortunate that some who pledge to uphold the commandments often show less love for their wives compared to those who don't share the same convictions by faith. (Eph 5:25, Col 3:19, Deut 5:10, 7:96, John 14:15, 21)

"And the Almighty Yah caused a deep sleep to fall upon Adam, and he slept: and he took one of his ribs, and closed up the flesh instead thereof; And the rib, which the Almighty Yah had taken from man, made he a woman, and brought her unto the man. And Adam said, This is now bone of my bones, and flesh of my flesh: she shall be called Woman, because she was taken out of Man." Gen. 2:21-23

"For the husband is the head of the wife, even as Christ is the head of the church: and he is the savior of the body." Eph. 5:23

The Priority Relationship

In the depths of the human experience, the husband/wife relationship doth emerge as the paramount bond. 'Tis of greater import than the sacred tie betwixt parent and child. Nay, even the bond 'twixt husband and wife and their own kin taketh a lower seat. 'Tis a relationship that doth tower above friendships forged beyond the home. Verily, the husband/wife relationship is the foremost relationship, surpassed only by our communion with the Most High God. It is more important than the husband's or wife's relationship with their own parents.

> **"Therefore, a man shall leave his father and
> mother and cleave unto his wife, and they shall be
> as one flesh." - Gen. 2:24**

The husband is bidden to set aside moments to delve into the depths of his wife's being and minister unto her soul. This injunction holdeth particular significance in the initial year of their union, therefore, when change and adaptation dost prevail [Deut. 24:5, Col. 3:19]. Their relationship is more important than the parent/child relationship. Let not the cares of life eclipse the joys of wedded bliss, for the courtship endures even after the marriage vows are spoken! Continue to revel in mirthful companionship [Ecc. 9:9].

Moreover, the husband is enjoined to be a beacon of encouragement. Tempting as it may be to criticize, complain, or wound with words, let it be known that such is not the manner in which Yeshua treateth His Church. Nay, He cherisheth it. And thus, a husband ought to treasure his wife. At every turn, he should build her up, stoke the fires of her spirit, and uplift her with unwavering support. He should be her most fervent advocate, taking righteous pride in her triumphs across all domains of life. This is one reason why the husband/wife relationship is the most important human relationship.

In this realm, the believer shall find wisdom by following the example of Yeshua's love for the Church. Let it be so, and a fruitful union shall be thine.

"Her offspring doth rise and extol her; her spouse likewise, he doth sing her praises." - Pr. 31:28

Yet another duty bestowed upon the husband is to be the lover of his wife. He must attend to her carnal desires and fulfill her needs. The act of lovemaking is an offering, wherein one's concern is focused on the satisfaction of the wife rather than the pursuit of personal gratification. The husband must grasp that his wife doth perceive the realm of intimacy through a different lens, and varied means shall minister unto her desires. Let him be gentle and kind, never too haughty to inquire of his wife's yearnings. It is recommended to consult Christian literature characterized by quality content and intricate descriptions to help satisfy sexual intimacy, such as "Act of Marriage", "Intended for Pleasure", "Love & Respect", and "Wired for Love". Pay attention: Seeking to improve the intimacy of marriage by engaging in explicit movies (Rated R) or similar inappropriate nudity content is a lustful action that causes significant damage to the sacred union of spiritual connection.

"And they were both unclothed, the man and his wife, and felt no shame." - Gen. 2:25

"The wife hath not power over her own body, but the husband: and likewise, the husband hath not power over his own body, but the wife." - 1 Cor. 7:4

The intent of this treatise is not to cast condemnation, but rather to stir the soul to action revealed by faith. Should our union fall short of its divine purpose, it is incumbent upon us to shoulder the weight of responsibility, seeking solace in precepts, psalms, hymns, and diligently implementing them. We may find it necessary to humbly implore the forgiveness of our beloved for our past transgressions. Servant Leaders are those adorned with humility. Then and only then, by manifesting a transformation towards Holy husbandry, shall we men prove the authenticity of our repentance. May the Most High God aid us, for with Him, all things are attainable, yet devoid of His grace, failure lurks as an inevitability.

But what course must a man take when his wife resists his leadership? Should he endeavor to compel her submission? How, then, doth Yeshua handle His Church when it strays from His path? He persisteth in His guidance, without compromise of divine precepts, seeking not compliance through coercion. He continueth to love and provide for His Church, revealing His devotion through unwavering faithfulness and tender care, even when His Church doth not merit such benevolence. Violence and manipulation find no place in His quest to elicit obedience from His Church. Verily, the predicament is arduous, yet let the deeds of Yeshua with His Church serve as a guide, unveiling the principles that govern such affairs.

Most wives shall not balk at the notion of submission when assured that their husbands faithfully tread the path ordained by the Most High God, exerting their utmost efforts for the welfare of their wives and households. Only if the wife persists in her wrongful actions with the deliberate intention of compromising or jeopardizing the relationship; does it merit a dissolution according to the holy commandments such an option of divorce becomes available.

No husband is bound to a union with a woman who consciously pursues a life steeped in sin. (Matthew 19:9)

Lastly, doth the role of the husband differ between believers and those estranged from the faith? Nay, the standards set by YAH remain unaltered across every realm of existence for all of His creation. Sin is the mark of separation from YAH. Just as Cain's sinful character made him a marked man of sin. A sinner dwells in a life of sin continuously. Alienation from YAH makes us sinful beings. We may have fallen short of the glory of YAH, yet whoever draws near with a pure heart to confess for forgiveness is granted mercy to be pardoned unto kingdom come by the impeccable standard of grace exemplified by Yeshua.

Nevertheless, empowered by the Holy Spirit, we must aspire to reach for the pinnacle. Let us never be content with ourselves but to strive for perfection of heart, mind, and soul. A man's commitment is to love his very best as his dedication to marriage is seen of his deeds of love demonstrated towards wife.

The Husband's Sacred Duty in Matrimony

Title: "The Sacred Duty of a Believer: A Tale of Love, Leadership, and Devotion"

Chapter 1: The Divine Calling

"In the realm of matrimony, a man is entrusted with a noble calling, one that bears the weight of responsibility and profound meaning. As a believer, his role transcends that of a mere husband, for he is called to be a leader, a protector, and a provider in his sacred union."

Chapter 2: The Virtues of a Responsible Husband

"Leadership, the cornerstone of a responsible husband's journey, is not demonstrated through dominance or control, but through love and servitude. By setting values that foster unity within the family, he sows the seeds of peace and joy, reaping a bountiful harvest in the abode he calls home."

"The husband's role as a spiritual covering for his family is of paramount importance. Through heartfelt prayers, he creates a sanctuary of divine protection, shielding his loved ones from the perils of the world. The husband who embraces this duty shall unfurl a banner of security under the watchful eye of the Most High God."

"Provision, both material and spiritual, is the hallmark of a responsible husband. Providing for the essential needs of his household is his sacred duty. As the Scriptures decree, 'But if anyone does not provide for his own, and especially for those of his household, he has denied the faith and is worse than an unbeliever' (1 Timothy 5:8)."

Chapter 3: The Act of Love and Service

"To truly serve one's wife is to provide for her in every sense of the word. The responsible husband not only attends to the material needs of his family but also takes the initiative to nourish his wife's spiritual well-being. By modeling Holy Spirit (character), the image of YAH can be fulfilled, praying together, studying to apply the Scriptures for self-improvement, self-development, and offering words of encouragement, he fulfills his role as a servant-leader in the eyes of the Most High God."

Chapter 4: Embracing the Divine Order

"The divine order established by the Most High God sets forth the husband as the head of the wife, not as a dictator but as a loving guide. In the words of the apostle Paul, 'Wives, be subject to your own husbands, as to the Lord... Husbands, love your wives, just as Christ also loved the church and gave Himself up for her' (Ephesians 5:22-25)."

"Let it be known that being the head does not imply dominance or superiority, but rather a selfless devotion to the well-being of one's wife. In the eyes of the Most High God, all believers stand as equals, for 'there is neither Jew nor Greek, slave nor free, male nor female, for you are all one in Yeshua (Galatians 3:28)."

Chapter 5: Honoring and Cherishing

"To honor one's wife is to respect her dignity and safeguard her privacy. The responsible husband refrains from gossip or disparaging remarks, building trust and upholding the sanctity of their bond. By embracing good behavior and maintaining a gentle spirit, he exemplifies the love of Yeshua in his actions."

Chapter 6: The Power of Unconditional Love

"Unconditional love, the hallmark of a responsible husband, mirrors the love of Yeshua for His Church. To love one's wife unconditionally is to cherish her worth as a gift from the Most High God. By constantly affirming her value, respect, and love, the husband fills her emotional tank, fostering a deep and lasting connection."

Chapter 7: Patience and Togetherness

"Patience, a virtue to be cherished, strengthens the marital bond

In moments when differences arise, the responsible husband accepts his wife as she is, addressing concerns with grace and kindness. Rather than dwelling on flaws, he focuses on the positive qualities that kindle love. Through quality time, open conversations, and shared aspirations, the couple nurtures their relationship, weaving a tapestry of togetherness."

Chapter 8: The Joy of Servanthood

"As the greatest example of servanthood, Yeshua washed the feet of His disciples, revealing the heart of a true leader. In emulation of His divine example, the responsible husband becomes a servant to his wife. By actively engaging in family matters, seeking her opinion, and striking a balance between parenthood and husbandhood, he uplifts and supports his cherished partner."

Chapter 9: Understanding and Meeting Needs

"To serve one's wife wholeheartedly is to understand and fulfill her needs. The responsible husband delves into her desires, fears, and burdens, striving to alleviate them. By attentively listening, he lessens her worries, lightens her load, and fosters an environment where her dreams can flourish. In recognizing and nurturing her gifts and talents, he empowers her to shine brightly in her endeavors."

Epilogue: The Eternal Reward

"To be a leader, a lover, and a servant is to surrender oneself to the precious gift bestowed by the Most High God—a wife. By laying down one's life for her, the faithful servant will find solace and fulfillment in the presence of Yeshua. And on the day of judgment, the voice of the Most High God will resound, proclaiming, 'Well done, thou good and faithful servant.'"

Through the captivating journey of this best-selling novel, readers will embark on a transformative exploration of love, marriage, and devotion, rediscovering the timeless wisdom encapsulated in the sacred texts and witnessing the profound impact a responsible believer can have on his family, society, and his own spiritual growth.

9 Ways to Make Marriage Passionate

Italians and people of many other Mediterranean countries bear an almost overt disdain for the clock. Rarely do they display a sense of urgency, instead embracing openness and hospitality towards unexpected visitors.

In stark contrast, Americans, burdened by their fast-paced lives, possess little room for spontaneity. They greet unannounced visits from friends not with joy but with irritation, their minds preoccupied with the ever-growing to-do list. Westerners compile endless lists, while Mediterraneans savor moments and indulge in love.

The essence of attunement, in essence, revolves around paying meticulous attention to one another. It entails diverting our focus from the multitude of distractions that clamor for our attention. It requires us to wholeheartedly tend to the love of our lives, even if only for a few moments each day.

We achieve this by engaging our eyes, body language, and the way we prioritize unhurried time together. Through affirmations, compliments, and uplifting gestures, we empower our partners, fostering their happiness as men and women. (If unsure about the words that bring them contentment, inquire!) It also necessitates closer introspection, nourishing our senses and allowing passion to arise and flow naturally. We appreciate our inner selves and present ourselves in a manner that radiates uniqueness, elegance, mirth, and allure. Regularly, we remain fully present for our beloveds, engaging them in proactive ways that indulge their senses.

1. Pay heed to the art of subtle touch.

Men, try placing your hand on the small of your wife's back as you guide her through a doorway. Place your hand over hers while driving, or tenderly bring her hand to your lips for a kiss. Women, gently caress the back of your man's neck while he drives, or rest your head upon his shoulder as you watch the evening's entertainment.

2. Envision a reunion akin to a first date.

Arrange a rendezvous at a coffee shop or café amidst the day's activities, or meet for a glass of wine after work, immersing yourselves in the enchantment of two individuals deeply enamored with one another.

3. Bestow compliments that affirm each other's masculinity or femininity.

Wives, speak words that kindle your man's sense of masculinity! ("I admire the way you assert yourself during meetings." "You are an extraordinary lover. It was truly remarkable.") Men, aid your beloved in embracing her womanhood! ("Your beauty, when bathed in sunlight near the window, leaves me breathless." "I adore your tenderness with our children.")

4. Maintain ample room in your lives for lingering.

If possible, reserve a portion of your weekends to savor unscheduled time together. Establish a habitual happy hour (even if only half an hour in duration) after work, where you can bask in each other's company on the porch during summer or snuggle on the couch or in a bubble bath.

5. Women, cherish your inner beauty.

Reflect upon the wisdom imparted by Sophia Loren, urging you to believe in your unparalleled beauty. Never forsake this aspect of your being. The confidence radiating from a woman who treasures the beauty bestowed upon her by the Most High God is utterly irresistible.

6. Men, endeavor to listen to or peruse books that inspire or teach you something new.

Delve into literature that delves deeper, provoking new questions within your soul. When the moment is opportune, and you and your beloved find yourselves lingering together—whether on a walk or upon the porch before supper—share the thoughts that these texts have evoked. Seek her opinion, listen attentively to her response, and demonstrate your appreciation for her insights and perspectives.

7. Laugh together whenever possible.

Laughter, one of the world's most undervalued aphrodisiacs, has the power to connect souls. Partake in amusing films, cartoons, or share a delightful YouTube video that you know will bring joy to your beloved. Do not hesitate to recount a humorous tale about yourself, for revealing our flaws through humor serves as a profound means of connecting with our soulmate.

8. **Integrate gratitude into your daily habits by expressing gratitude through words of thanks.**

You will be astounded by how these two simple words, generously bestowed, fortify the bonds of love and romance. Attempt this: every evening, between dinner and the extinguishing of lights, while you are together, express gratitude to the one you love for at least one thing they have done or one aspect of their being that blesses your life.

9. **Embrace emotional openness, particularly regarding positive and tender sentiments.**

If a surge of gratitude for the day's beauty, the love of your wife, or the adorable nature of your children overwhelms you, do not keep it to yourself. Utter it aloud, infusing your words with energy and passion.[3]

---

3 Stephen and Misty Arterburn. (2017) 9 Ways to Feed the Passion in Your Marriage. https://www.familylife.com/articles/topics/marriage/staying-married/romance-and-sex/9-ways-to-feed-the-passion-in-your-marriage/ Accessed 2017

A Father's Role

In truth, a Father of the family holds the esteemed position of a true Father within the Community. A father assumes the role of a household leader, and his unwavering leadership extends to the neighborhood, fostering a tranquil and harmonious community. When a family flourishes, the community regards them as a beacon of virtue, and the Father, as the head of the household, bears both the accolades and burdens.

Researchers have discovered that the love—or rejection—of both mothers and fathers equally impacts children's behavior, self-esteem, emotional stability, and mental well-being. "However, in certain cases, the absence of a father's love appears to play a more significant role in children's struggles with personality and psychological adjustment, delinquency, and substance abuse. On the other hand, the presence of a father's love can greatly enhance children's sense of well-being and contribute to their emotional and physical health. Children who have fathers actively involved in their lives demonstrate better learning capabilities, higher self-esteem, and fewer indications of depression compared to children without fathers." It has also been observed that children who perceive their fathers as supportive experience a greater sense of social acceptance and exhibit fewer signs of depression.

"Father involvement holds tangible significance, be it in intellectual development, sex-role development, or psychological growth. Most children thrive when they enjoy a close and affectionate relationship with their fathers, especially when fathers reside alongside them."

A father's character profoundly influences a child's future. If a child witnesses their father succumbing to anger, they may deem such behavior acceptable. Thus, a tremendous responsibility rests upon a father's shoulders. However, why is there such emphasis on fathers? What about mothers?

The role of a mother in a child's life has long been acknowledged, but humans possess a unique distinction. In the animal kingdom, it is solely the mothers who care for their offspring. The father's role is confined to procreation, showing no further concern for the young. However, humans diverge from this pattern, as fathers also assume responsibility. Only when love and righteousness prevail within a family can true happiness be attained.

Mothers often exhibit tenderness towards their children, yet the children also require firm discipline. This discipline can be provided by the father. If the mother adopts a strict approach, the father can embody leniency, thereby complementing the mother's role.

Parenting is a collaborative effort. An ancient African proverb asserts that it takes a village to raise a child. While a child is influenced and shaped by the entire society, no two individuals play a more crucial role in this process than the parents. Both the mother and father hold significant and distinct responsibilities in parenting. Let us not confuse "parenting" with the "duties of a parent." The "tasks" involved in raising a child can be shared equally and interchangeably between both parents. However, parenting surpasses these tasks. It encompasses the promotion of a child's well-being by nurturing their physical, intellectual, emotional, and social development. Read further to explore the different roles a mother plays as the primary teacher in effectively raising a child.

Children are inclined to learn, but not solely from what is taught to them. They acquire knowledge primarily through emulation of their parents rather than mere words. Once, a father was tending to his garden when he was unexpectedly summoned away, leaving his work unfinished. Observing his father, the son picked up the abandoned axe and heedlessly felled a fruit-bearing tree that his father had diligently nurtured. The child's mother was alarmed, fearing her son would face severe punishment from his father. When the father returned and beheld the fallen tree, he inquired about the responsible party, and the son truthfully admitted his actions. The father embraced him and explained that henceforth, the boy must seek his father's guidance on which trees to cut and which to preserve. The mother questioned her husband as to why he had not chastised the boy. The man responded that he refrained from punishing the child because he had spoken the truth. To discipline him would have conveyed the wrong message, leading the boy to believe that honesty does not yield favorable outcomes. Thus, a wise father can guide his child toward becoming a responsible and honest individual.

Fathers play important roles in their children's lives.

1. Priest / Spiritual Leader

"As much as I am able, I ensure that we are a family that lives in accordance with the commandments and will of the Most High God," Francis elucidates. "This enables us to be more attuned to Yah's love for us. On a deeper level, this role grants me the opportunity to guide my children's lives towards Yeshua, especially during their formative years."

"The Most High God has bestowed upon the father a uniquely special role within the family," he continues. "For the family is akin to a sacred sanctuary, and the father bears a vital responsibility in fostering its spiritual life. He must lead the family in prayer, be it before and after meals, the imparting of blessings upon the children before they embark upon their daily endeavors, or the sharing of Yah's divine word."

2. Protector

"Men must remain vigilant even concerning the most basic matters of security that affect our lives," he asserts. "Protection encompasses not only physical safety but also emotional security, financial stability, and other aspects."

Fathers are duty-bound not only to safeguard their children physically from any danger or harm but also to shield them morally and spiritually," Francis explains. "Studies have revealed that many of society's present challenges, such as learning disabilities, emotional and behavioral issues leading to juvenile delinquency, premarital relations, drug abuse, and crime, can be traced back to the absence of a father due to broken marriages. The world today teems with countless forces that assail and erode the fabric of family life and values."

3. Provider

"I have always believed that the role of a provider should not be dictated solely by cultural norms," he reflects. "To provide for one's family is an integral part of the vow a man makes on his wedding day."

The father, therefore, assumes the responsibility not only for the family's spiritual needs but also their material and emotional well-being. "He must ensure that he possesses the means to sustain these needs," Francis affirms. "Together with his wife, he must impart to their children the wisdom of living within their means, while also exemplifying through practical means the values of financial responsibility and independence."

4. Teacher

The father assumes the role of a teacher to his children. "It would be unjust if children were to remain bereft of learning from their fathers," Francis insists. "Whether imparting academic knowledge or engaging in activities within the home, children must always receive instruction from their fathers alongside their mothers."

"A father opens his child's eyes to the world; through him, his children experience the essence of life and the manner in which it ought to be lived," he emphasizes.

Don, a devoted father, finds immense fulfillment in expanding his children's minds and hearts, preparing them for life's journey. The inquisitive questions of his two older daughters, such as "Why?" and "What's that, Daddy?" resonate constantly within his ears. "As a father, it is my duty to teach my children about our faith," he states. "I must be capable of answering their questions when we are in the presence of Yah and demonstrate to them through my actions how a person should lead a virtuous life."

"Fathers must also instill hope within their children. To reassure them that after a tempestuous storm, a new day will dawn. That after a conflict, they can still forge the deepest bonds of friendship," he adds. "And above all, to love them unconditionally. While I may guide, correct, and instruct them, at the end of the day, my love for them as my children knows no bounds."

5. Playmate

"My children often express their delight when I am present, as it grants them the opportunity to engage in play. From launching paper airplanes to partaking in board games and indulging in hide-and-seek within the confines of our humble abode, I can effortlessly assume the role of their playmate," Don beams.

6. Companion

Fathers must also allocate time for their families. "I recall reading a book years ago titled 'The Five Key Habits of Wise Fathers,' which stated that children perceive love through the gift of time," Francis shares. "Fathers must maximize their presence during significant moments in their children's lives, be it birthdays, recitals, school performances, sporting events, parent-child meetings, church activities, academic accolades, graduations, or engagements."

Fathers must remain actively involved in their children's lives, even when they have families of their own. "Fathers should invest time in assisting their children with their own offspring," he asserts.

7. Trainer

"How does one accomplish this, Daddy?" and "How does that melody go?" resonate as common queries from his children.

8. Talent developer

Proclamations from his daughters, such as "I can accurately kick the ball towards the goal, Daddy!" and "Daddy, I also desire to play the piano!" ignite a profound sense of pride within Don.

9. Procreator

"The father is also a participant in the act of procreation," Ramon declares. "Both the husband and wife have been bestowed with a sacred and divine role - to contribute to the creation of new life. Therefore, the act of procreation within the bounds of marriage assumes a sacred nature. Sex is not a mere commodity; rather, parents bear the primary responsibility of teaching their children that sex is a divine gift from Yah - something to be cherished, respected, and protected."

10. Servant Leader

The father serves as the head and servant of the family. "He must lead by example, demonstrating his roles and responsibilities to his wife and children," Francis expounds. "While the father assumes the position of authority and leadership within the family, he must exercise these roles with a servant's heart. He serves selflessly, without expecting anything in return, and must also possess the humility[4] to acknowledge his own limitations and vulnerabilities."

Indeed, fulfilling all these roles is an arduous and demanding task. Let us extend our positive energy to all the fathers out there, particularly on the Sabbath day, and exhibit our unwavering support and encouragement to the fathers in our lives!

---

[4] Pediatric Academic Societies. (2000). Importance of Fathers in Children's Lives. https://www.newswise.com/articles/importance-of-fathers-in-childrens-lives. Tina Santiago-Rodriguez. (2012) The 10 Roles a Father Plays in his Child's Life. https://www.smartparenting.com.ph/life/love-relationships/the-call-to-fatherhood-what-being-a-father-is-all-about

May these insights inspire men to become more actively engaged in the care of their children, thus leading to the holistic well-being of the entire family. Men are called to love their wives as they love their own flesh; therefore, it is unwise to enter into a union with a woman who does not wholly ignite desire within them.

An Honorable Man Stands

The Fall of a Man is His Ego
A woman is not a man's equal
Can a man be the savior of his people?
A good woman brings out the best in man.

A man is far more superior in his right mind
Never is a man broke in his dignity,
Honor is his responsibility to himself
Self-control of appetite, a discipline
Never allows anyone to possess his soul

Maintain composure at all times
Even the psychological
discipline of woman and child
A goal for progression
Avoids evil eye, gossip, and jealously

Principles of Union

Why should men and women unite? Besides the heterosexual relationship of procreation; is it for the good of mankind to continue with life. What principles should man and woman unite?

A successful marriage has to share the same principles which are expected to evolve over time as knowledge is sought after for a better quality of life. A marriage that does not evolve wears away the strength of marriage to carry the back of the other.

Avoid the marriage of a habitual drunkard set in a way of not to consider another's viewpoint.

Difficult is it to confront a habitual offender of one's action in question; having a history of doing things a familiar way for quite some time. The wise approach is to address only matters of a mutual interaction (pertaining to self) and disregard all others to prevent possible turmoil as an outcome of suspicion. Dead to argue the point, but let the matter be known peaceably. If there's any friction, leave without holding on to any baggage one dishes out to burden you by the scornful remarks directed from negative thoughts of confusion. Thinking negatively of another can lead to a selfishness hidden from plain view if not released from the mind of consciousness.

Whoever carries a grudge against another to bring up dead matters after one has made amends is a stumbling block for every occasion an issue is brought to surface for moving forward. The grudge carrier is like a stubborn mule set in a way that is uncooperative; using the past incident(s) as a reason to not move forward as the ego of conceit does not allow them to reconcile after the approach of forgiveness. No matter the gift or words one may say to do, the ego of pride resides deeply rooted in one's heart not to release its victim from one's venom.

Flee from conceit, a hidden selfishness is a sign of immaturity. Spare yourself the agony of marriage, as it may be a sign observed of others before it encounters you. This selfishness is hidden from plain sight as you may be blamed for one's misfortune.

Relationships: An Honor of Commitment

Have you been in the presence of honor to know and feel what it looks is like? Who do you know living with honor among you? Whatever thoughts come to mind make it part of your attire. Truly, what a privilege it is to be in the presence of consistency. Specially to see the way of life chosen for the greater good of moral values implemented in committed relationship.

The way to find the heart of a person is to learn what restrictions are worthy of sacrifice concerning one's wellbeing. You know that you have found a friend when you can behold what is truthfully within the eyes. Always finish your thoughts so that you accomplish all, leaving nothing undone as you respect that of your neighbor. Disable the unfruitful or negative sentence from your social existence and you shall multiply exceedingly in the land you dwell.

The following points illustrated are to warn and hold accountable the individual who may not recognize signs in relationships as things are taken for granted out of convenience.

Be careful to never live on the edge of bad relationships only to suffer a predicament of great penalty. As one does not confront the issues of a bad relationship; the wounds remain as scars of hurt growing deeper and deeper as resentment becomes a reproach of shame.

Engage in a healthy relationship that confesses faults before one another so that positive behavior is the result that takes accountability for one's actions. Do not place your thoughts before another's; but consider what is spoken in your presence so that inclusion of each voice is respected.

Be careful to never dominate or force your decisions upon another so that one's life is lived through the eyes of one. Rather than criticize and conceal your feelings of hurt and dislike; make known your concerns to the party of disapproval to express how you feel. Bringing negative thoughts to any situation can make one not feel safe even comfortable expressing oneself.

Be careful to never defeat the mentality of anyone to become a victim solely depended on you rather than to trust self. Is it not senseless to choose words that tear down the wall of character even one's ego to make another fear you? The intent of a man's heart can be felt through his choice of words and demeanor expressed. Also, bad vibrations are felt when negatively imposed acts of intimidation and devices of control such as to make one subject to another's authority. Where patience is at end and the victim has no room for mercy; shall not the victim be destroyed in the presence of wrath as any bystander? It is wise to resolve tension and not to provoke one's hurt so that wrath does not result from the anger of frustration.

Be careful to never interfere with personal liberty so that one is not made the object of oppression. Encourage the pursuit of one's own interest without unsolicited advice; so that the experience of making mistakes and learning from others is valued in an individual's growth of independence. Spend time to focus on revealing who you are through what makes you sad and glad when alone and in company of another.

Taking responsibility for one's own actions can be an identity issue if past behaviors are not recognized the consequence is the beginning of an unhealthy relationship. A healthy relationship can be supported by resolving the offenses committed in accountability and having the emotional intelligence to not succumb negatively charged thoughts to an emotional outburst of hurt. If separation does not occur, a man or woman who is unable to express emotional hurt may lose self-control and lash out cruelty on the victim. When either is capable of expressing one's emotions; a relief of the circumstances that face them helps to maintain a healthy conscience of peace within.

The first role models of a family lie within the relationship of a man and woman union. It is good for every woman to be united with man, especially in raising up children. The authority and protection of every woman is the covering of her head, the man. A man's responsibility is to watch over the family that there be no broken family syndrome. A woman's responsibility is to nurture the family respecting the authority of the man. A man was designed to secure women in a committed relationship. However, when a man does what he wants a broken family is the result of a woman over extended or vice versa. A righteous role model holds accountable every man and woman from polluting the community starting at home. A divine source of authority observed of nature, shows the handy work of God is consistent throughout universe, laws are clearly seen to govern the whole creation.

A legacy role model allows families to invest time wisely in business for the expansion of creating an economy that governs itself. Taking action in this direction allows thoughts of creativity to manifest together. A humble support system managed from where the families live prospers in abundance to create wealth and unity. Order starts in the home that a man may have the support of his community defending injustice that mercy and truth prevail rather than a woman abandoned and without peace; scared from injury such as the loss of life nurtured.

Labor of Love for Reconciliation

What is worth your time to love for eternity and for a season? Somethings fade away from the heart because that's all its good for as others remain to serve your purpose of goodwill and happiness. Reconciliation is the health of consciousness to examine and grow from situations necessary to move on to the next season of our life.

There is a special element beyond love that is required for long term relationships. Our thoughts and feelings of love is ignorant as it is limited to what one understands. Today, a problem solver is not good enough to reconcile the emotion. There are many people hurting today who may not see the problem as it does not relate to the world in which is viewed. Therefore, we have to come equipped with a tool bag of emotional intelligence to handle inner personal relationships where much is at stake and condolence is needed. The emotional aspect deals with not only knowing the character of another, but also having an awareness that detects how you feel in respect of the character's vibe. The ability to be truthful with yourself and others is maturity that will allow the relationship to grow. Pretending, holding back, or deviating from what was agreed that nothing is wrong to prevent conflict is an immature relationship on the verge of sudden calamity. A happy relationship needs communication that feels good to each other. The medium of happy communication brings an attraction of joy to the relationship. Joy, peace, and love are high frequencies that allow one or many to create new or enhance existing relationships. High frequency relationships are able to move quickly in building new principles that may extend beyond the scope of one's family origin.

Most relationships are based on what one has observed as a child throughout young adulthood. The development of the ability to express feelings in any environment does not warrant the proper emotional intelligence if one is as a child subjected to the suppression of the authority present. Today for this reason have we many that are not fully developed mentally to handle the affairs of a family. The humble walk of life is not an easy journey to take. Having respect for the power of choice and gratitude for the experience that teaches explicitly without getting emotionally attached to problems. This walk of life requires great discipline of an inner peace that goes beyond the suppression of emotions and returns the situation to a calm state without interference as the authority in control. Think to serve rather than to be master, for through your service shall you be called master. A teacher ever a leader is a humble servant of the people to surround oneself with intellectual property without a since of ownership is love as the establishment of children.

Let your actions be true to you loving yourself. Your commitment to yourself is the biggest appreciation one can imagine. Taking action allows you to see the result in your life; this sense of accomplishment increases self-worth. Self-worth raises the esteem and awareness for the capability to be creative while setting limits as boundaries for accountability. There may be situations to where you may have to sacrifice what you have to leverage your time; the financial means gives you choices that can help you provide more wealth for yourself.

Desperate situations do not increase wealth but grieves your health, so do yourself a favor and walk away from things that devalue your time, money, and causes you stress. As you confront yourself in the mirror of business, don't be afraid to walk away from your old self for higher values that reinvent who you are so that your business is not compromised for your lack of conviction. Just The elders of a community are to hold accountable the members as much as the owner of business. Truly you see who people are for how they serve their community.

Quality of Reflection

What reminds you of who you are, the values shared, and the life you seek to fulfill?

Beautiful is to find one whom you can share all of your heart without circumspection. This value is priceless and a rare treasure to know that you are secure in all your ways without the hassle of worry to weary in one's inquiries of uncertainty. The heart and mind are the most prized possession beyond the looks of beauty. You can do so much more than one can imagine with another who is after your heart and mind to be one in the direction you pursue throughout eternity. The reflection of one's attitude can attest to the aptitude to discover and resolve issues in the course of action consciously and ignorantly.

A beautiful heart and mind give you so much liberty to do the impossible that it makes life very easy to make provisions for others in need of vital resources. Having a more satisfaction of heart, the relationship achieves a higher level of happiness than a commitment of promise that is irresistible to ever imagine departure.

Consider a key factor for any union to become a reality is to put aside differences for what is moral by nature. Cultural differences allow a union to embrace another world of discovery to adjust from ignorance to common sense. Polite manners receive the welcome of rebuke humbly from another who rightfully encounters a question of fault.

The beloved is loved in every way possible, knowing the merit of life suitable of a pure heart and mind. A healthy conscience allows grace to settle matters to avoid all selfishness from one's existence. Unity is love, the vibrant energy that knows there is nothing impossible that cannot be done.

The mirror quality of reflection is to see yourself within another. If one is unable to reflect who you are the trials of life will be endless and quite burdensome for you to endure. An alternative seeks separation to learn of the faults that broke the relationship's ability to share hearts perfectly in unity. If there can be reconciliation it is best to sever the relationship. Love is without prejudice, hate, conceit, jealousy, and envy which mostly stems from fear. True love will never do anything to hurt anyone no matter what one has done. Therefore, when you find it, you are secure in the one you are in union and vice versa. The greater love does not care to make material possessions a focus of comfort and can do without it no matter the crisis suffered. Love finds its way out of situations to escape the negative thoughts that curses progression, the hindrance to self if anyone else.

Freedom is the ambition of an unlimited potential to do whatever the heart desires with clarity to fulfill life's purpose. Commonly without focus, disengagement occurs from distractions driving away the potential to perform.

New desires help to focus on the potential beyond the imagination, especially the support of one's reflection in union. The one who is free takes accountability for all responses of action. Clarity is a peace of mind that allows one to create, without it one is all over the place in shambles.

Cultivate the Strong

What is the foundation of strength within your walls?

Cultivate what you know that grows strong as it takes a village to raise a child in a happy home.

An apple falls not too far from its tree as manners will take you further than money will.

Have respect for yourself and others, for where you come from, not to skip over what your ancestors instilled.

A brotherhood of counsel is found within a king. So be wise to how a queen adores to comfort, the man of her dreams.

The same is as a rock that does not move from its position.

Standing corrected from chastisement, never to return to the humiliation of a tarnished character.

The best parts of wisdom are hidden from the force within; beheld of honor to whom chooses to wield the light.

For a moment, what we don't know is what we discover to seek within ourselves the virtue of a true and faithful reality.

The answer that you find use it to your advantage, otherwise discard it in silence to cultivate the strong.

The Power of Choice

How much do you believe in yourself? You always have a choice in the matter, the only time there is no choice is when you have ran out of options or have not thought clearly of all the possibilities. Are you happy with the choices you have made at this point? Have you made any choices that you still regret? I cannot tell you to get over it, but I can tell you that if you have regretted your self-esteem is suppressed and you need redemption from this situation. You can always redeem your self-esteem from acts of generosity, the bigger the deed the bigger the redemption.

The power of choice is a healthy tool for the success of all relationships. Make your choice strong by the validation of intrapersonal or extra-personal values pertaining to the situation. Respect is the key component for decision preservation of another to assemble new ideas, creativity, and spontaneity. However, before choice is made on the behalf of two or more persons; it is wise to have a code of ethics (system of rules) for interaction to alleviate any misunderstanding of behavior. New knowledge is born when common knowledge is shared upon mutual agreeable thoughts for the power of choice and creativity to excel. Eliminate stress through collaboration to offset the pressure from one to many when many stakeholders are dependent upon the choice at hand. If the communication of the workload is found grievous at any time; unhealthy persons suffer within the relationship.

Overtime these situations experience burnout to jeopardize health. Therefore, a healthy approach could adjust ethics to reflect positive values that grow and develop quality relationships. Empathy and sympathy are an invaluable trait of emotional intelligence that heals wounds and restores balance. Compassion and mercy are invaluable as kindness and forgiveness leans together to flourish in harmony. Honorable and faithful are priceless qualities seen in mature relationships for appreciation that disallows distractions from interfering in the relationship. Consideration and moderation are most excellent for knowing one's limits of actions and thoughts; the act of discretion, and the taking heed of caution that many do not stumble for the sake of vanity.

Wisdom teaches the power of choice; yet without exposure to life's circumstances do we learn in trials of ignorance around others. Wisdom guards peace and chooses not to create or invest in a relationship that is hidden in mischief and has no room for consideration. Too many unpleasant circumstances make it difficult to maintain a relationship as it grows in agony. These particular relationships bring on stress to whom may choose to terminate all dealings. No matter what be calm, patience maintains discipline to set boundaries of respect without less interaction. The offender will eventually recognize what is important in the relationship and at some point move on.

Many interim/interrupt relationships are but for a season of time to take course around the universe giving all opportunity to know truly the value of life. Abusers who chose not to value life become a detriment to society as their wounds become another's burden of hurt that may lead to a tragedy. Do all you can do to ensure that all relationships continue and end in peace as healthy decisions enforce good counsel leave no risk for abuse to manifest! The power of choice in relationships is a healthy tool as the labor of love for reconciliation takes place in the hearts those making an effort of change for a common goal.

Qualities Instilled in A Child

Aren't children the most precious of all nature? They have a big heart, pure of love and possess the ability to change the world we live. Therefore, let them learn through observation and careful instruction rather than forceful methods that impair the psyche of their view of reality. The power of choice is important to all children as it defines their character to make sound decisions throughout their journey of life. Parents seek an honest and humble way of life to raise up wise children in harmony with nature.

Nurturing a child without prejudice is beautiful as the support to raise self-esteem and awareness is invaluable. Parents have oversight to provide a wealth of nourishment to a healthy mind that copes with feelings, a child's emotional needs. Parents, man and woman are necessary to foster healthy relationships throughout a child's development. If children learn to respect the dominant and submissive energy of authority, they shall become wise to mature with authority. Both parents not only provide guidance and protection of child's identity; but instill discipline within character to know their place in this world in search of greatness. For the sake of love, please do not use forceful measures to exert your presence above your children as a mechanism of control.

Children oppose or become what is revealed around them. Children reveal to their parent's things done right and wrong of their past doings. Wisdom has the man and woman who chooses to correct the wrong before the union of bringing forth children. Parents have the ability to show them who they are by what takes control of their day. If parents are not in control, neither will they be mentally or emotionally. Parents have a sound mind upon everything you do as children seek to be happy with you. Children are learning who and what it is they will be in society. Give them a mind of questioning to know a matter before any action proceeds. Children must have the instruction of a moral law to know how to treat others as they would be. Parents are responsible for teaching children universal laws of nature and local laws of government.

Parents be consistent to enforce values based on a code of ethics to raise mature children of a sound mind. A sound mind has clarity to elevate beyond those who have not a system of values. A child is noble to have a system of values of which they shall never fall; unless they depart from it.

Love has many ways of discipline that can correct what is wrong. Parents are guides for discipline to balance energy; so, one does not occupy the center of attention to dominate the relationship in dictating what decisions are made as the other resides on standby. A healthy development is without a dictatorship that rules over relationships but identifies the traits of a character with purpose. The following helps to introduce a child to identify character traits.

Identify with Parents	The personality, background, and historical information that a child receives from both parents are important in developing a freewill way of life from inherited customs and beliefs to form a system of values. Avoid rearing up a child into servitude as it creates inner conflict with one's purity to be held hostage in a controlled environment. Confusion is without reason that a child does not have a perspective for involvement other than what was provided.
Identify Relationships	Relationships are important for a child to grasp within one's development; so that impact of unforeseen events impairs their growth around others is minimal. However, the difference in a child's development is generally centered on what is learned from healthy and unhealthy situations. Children are diverse in learning; therefore, it is wise to caution with instruction that gauges interaction rather than to shelter them from negative situations without hope of resolution; but to teach them what can be learned in normal and dysfunctional relationships. Equipping them with the power of choice to decide which relationships are healthy to entertain.
Identify with Health	Teaching a child to know the vital signs of life in nature has a wealthy outlook on life for survival. Health has always been determined based on the knowledge one has acquired of nature's minerals, nutrients, and resources vital to life.
Exposure to Cultures	Give a child exposure to diverse cultures for familiarity of coping skills and respect of feelings to avoid trespass that keep the soul liberated freely accepted
Principles of choice	There are ways in which a child must learn the manners of respect regarding others. Besides, choice it is an important matter of decision that a child must make on one's own. The selection of choice as an opportunity throughout the development of a child's life for governing self develops strong character. Yet out of respect for the parents' principles and discipline a child should be aware of the consequences in result of the option chosen as more choice is granted never take away one's options as a punishment.
Creativity & Imagination	A spark of genius in seen in those whose ideas have not been tampered with for inspiration, creation, and imagination of new works to be presented.

Decisions Making & Thinking	Maturity gives more options to a child knowing that one has the insight to make careful decisions on a consistent basis as a form of moral strength. Whether learning from the mistakes of others or consequence of actions made. On the Contrary, a child without options is subjected to the circumstances of a controlled environment. Limited options do not sit well with children of low morale when amongst their peers.
Accountability of Humanity	It is necessary to take on learning roles of responsibility. A child's development should be one that learns from responsibility. If not learned the end result for all actions performed within the universe are selfishly biased. Whether towards nature or any form of life; the care that takes place in a child's development determines whether they will carefully consider the existence of life wherever they may be present.
Personality & Esteem	Give a child freedom to develop personality as self-esteem and confidence flourishes, the power of choice becomes easier to grasp. Their self-esteem to create grows in abundance knowing what they do makes them happy to be fearless.
Purity of Heart	The innocent child knows no wrong as wrong is learned from the environment. Keep the chastity of youth alive in the thoughts that one may remain innocent. Teach the consequence of action from learned behaviors indecent to cultural or moral values.

Creating a Strong Family: Leaving a Noble Legacy for Your Children

1. Lead by Example:

Demonstrate the character traits you wish to instill in your children. Remember, "more is caught than taught." Whether it's honesty, service, or an authentic relationship with Yeshua, your actions speak louder than words. Your life is a powerful influence on theirs.

2. Consistency is Key:

Establish and uphold consistent rules and consequences. Challenges to your authority are opportunities for teaching. Consistency creates security, helping children understand boundaries. A stable environment builds their confidence in your leadership. Consistency now fosters respect later.

3. Align Choices with YAH's Word:

Make intentional choices that align with YAH's Word and the legacy you desire. Avoid impulsive decisions based on convenience. Small choices collectively shape values. Be mindful of what you watch, your priorities, and how you spend your free time. Your decisions contribute to the family's values.

4. Prayer and Reflection:

Pray for your family regularly and reflect on your successes and failures. Define your parenting goals and journal about them. Setting clear goals and praying for your family aligns your actions with your aspirations. Parenting requires wisdom, courage, patience, grace, and forgiveness.

Remember, being a parent is a challenging but rewarding journey. Building a set apart (holy) family demands intentional effort and a commitment to fostering an environment of love, wisdom, and faith.

Many people today suffer from bad relationships and may not consider a conversation about how to choose the right relationship. This is a big deal which is of great importance to do so. What is the goal of a relationship? Is it to achieve a greater happiness, is it short-term or long-term? Today, because the stability of families is at stake, I decided to choose this topic centered on a long-term relationship. There are many benefits to a long-term relationship which will be discussed in the next chapter. Generally, ideas of this relationship include: Building financial freedom for legacy (generational wealth), sharing a lifetime of great memories, introducing values into society, or to create your own reality. Whichever brings you happiness match up with a partner for your success.

Choose the Right Relationship

Name three goals you have in common to accomplish over the next 5 years.

When you think of a entering a new relationship what comes to mind, Besides physical or mental attraction?

A relationship should be considered as an investment of time, energy, and effort for growing your success. When choosing a relationship, it is good to conduct a future goals assessment evaluating the number of differences and commonalities that would potentially grow you closer or further apart. If you don't cut your losses early you will surely pay for it later. Today, our discussion covers three points for choosing a relationship with the potential for success plus stats on marriage stacked against your relationship. Don't be a statistic.

The first is to examine the awareness of your partner's consciousness such as moral conduct, beliefs and values, awareness of senses, intelligence, and decision making.

Remember if you have children, you are responsible for what is introduced into society. What is imagined of your best self in the future ought to be the image your children observes of you. Create a journal and revisit your entries for what image you decide to portray as family values? Greatness doesn't happen overnight; therefore we are in continuous improvement. Goals established from personal development helps "The man in the mirror" to "Take a look at yourself and make a change." Relationships vested in each other ought to consider learning their partner's strengths and weaknesses. This opens a healthy channel of communication and awareness for personal development.

Stats on 1st Marriage

The number #1 statistic why most marriages fail is due to a breakdown in communication. Over time a breakdown of communication occurs from lack of fulfillment to have each other's needs met.

"The average first marriage that ends in divorce lasts about 8 years.

Almost 50 percent of all marriages in the United States will end in divorce or separation. Researchers estimate that 41 percent of all first marriages end in divorce. 60 percent of second marriages end in divorce. 73 percent of all third marriages end in divorce. Every 13 seconds, there is one divorce in America. Over a 40-year period, 67 percent of first marriages terminate.

The second is a strong pursuit of desires to push each other to accomplish the same vision. As partners you ought to have the same goals in mind to achieve a greater life of peace. The more success you have together in all areas of life contributes to a greater happiness called joy. Growing the relationship stronger with happy memories: merits honor having formed a greater trust and respect for a mutual bond of love. This union now becomes more precious than anything else.

Among all Americans 18 years of age or older, whether they have been married or not, 25 percent have gone through a marital split. 15 percent of adult women in the United States are divorced or separated today, compared with less than one percent in 1920."[5]

Third, personality allows growth in every area without criticism to condemn. Depending on how familiar you are with yourself you may choose the wrong personality that clashes with your decision to build your dreams. Personalities are influenced by many factors of exposure: For instance, the environment, growth from childhood to adulthood, blood type, and what authority of guidance one looks to develop self.

[5] Wilkinson & Finkbeiner Family Law Attorneys. (2021, January 1). DIVORCE STATISTICS: OVER 115 STUDIES, FACTS AND RATES FOR 2020 Retrieved from https://www.wf-lawyers.com/divorce-statistics-and-facts

Because these factors of experience conditions the heart, mind, and soul; a partner entering a relationship has to consider if the lifestyle of discipline and personality bonds well for a natural vibe that feels safe and comfortable to not have intentions questioned for what had been done or in the act of doing. Otherwise without observational study, questions of differences and many explanations are needed to justify the act of something taking place. Because every moment is not a teaching moment of life; high performers may experience a slowdown of progress. Therefore, chose your partner wisely to know their personality is suitable for yours.

"According to the Pentagon, the military divorce rate is 3.4 percent in the 2013 fiscal year. However, the rate was significantly higher in military women at 7.2 percent. The Divorce rate among enlisted troops was 3.8 percent. Among officers, the divorce rate was 1.9 percent. The Air Force has the highest divorce rate among enlisted troops of any military branch at 4.3 percent. The divorce rate among U.S. Navy Seals is over 90 percent."[6]

These statistics you must consider when choosing the right relationship as the cards of divorce are greatly stacked against your success as we see in module#7 the circumstances lead to poverty if not thought out carefully.

---

[6] Wilkinson & Finkbeiner Family Law Attorneys. (2021, January 1). DIVORCE STATISTICS: OVER 115 STUDIES, FACTS AND RATES FOR 2020 Retrieved from https://www.wf-lawyers.com/divorce-statistics-and-facts

Responsibility of Commitment

Now that you have chosen your relationship, you have a responsibility of commitment to ensure that the odds of divorce stacked again you do not prevail. What we are about to discuss now are four areas of dedication consisting of the art of communication and taking affirmative action to overcome divorce.

Choosing the right relationship is important for esteem to be felt mutually. Let's begin with how support and empowerment is achieved for healthy progression. When there is a need to push, assist, or esteem your partner to achieve a goal; some relief is felt as gladness makes the heart happy for appreciation. Support and empowerment keep the relationship thriving and your partner is inspired to do more by the attraction of your positive energy.

The next responsibility deals with overcoming past and present obstacles to accomplish the vision of future goals. If a relationship takes the approach to improve communication, health, and work habits; what can we expect? The formation of patterns for success and overtime a greater expression of self is made manifest. The main goal here is self-mastery so that no obstacle would be a hindrance to your relationship. Whether working alone or together the goals are completed and the vision is made a reality.

Depending on the experiences one incurred of the past and present; healing may need to take course as a way to nurture weakness to strength. No one should want to continue suffering in a relationship from anything that can be cured. Therefore, it is your moral responsibility to get help immediately so that healing takes place to get back on track with completing your goals envisioned. Getting help or providing relief physically, mentally, or emotionally is nurturing weakness to strength so that you can thrive as a team feeling light and more energetic for success.

Last of all teamwork makes the dream work. You chose the relationship for a dream of what you envisioned of your future. Therefore, it is your responsibility to see it through to the end by fulfilling all that you agreed upon until the day of completion. A solidified team has unity at the core of its beginning, no quitters on board, only winners who make things happen no matter what without excuses.

Benefits for entering a relationship: emotional and financial stability, increase positive psychological state of mind. Longer life, stress reduction, help fulfill purpose of life, greater chance of survivors, support, healing, teamwork.

Lack of commitment is the most common reason given by divorcing couples according to a recent national survey. Here are the reasons given and their percentages: "Lack of commitment 73% Argue too much 56% Infidelity 55% Married too young 46% Unrealistic expectations 45% Lack of equality in the relationship 44% Lack of preparation for marriage 41% Domestic Violence or Abuse 25%"[7]

These statistics you must consider when choosing the right relationship as the cards of divorce are greatly stacked against your success as we see in module#7 the circumstances lead to poverty if not thought out carefully.

---

[7] Wilkinson & Finkbeiner Family Law Attorneys. (2021, January 1). DIVORCE STATISTICS: OVER 115 STUDIES, FACTS AND RATES FOR 2020. Retrieved from https://www.wf-lawyers.com/divorce-statistics-and-facts

Relationship Upgrade and Maintenance

Every relationship needs attention, love, and affection to feel alive for something worthwhile. This unspoken affirmation connects hearts and minds to the core truth necessary to do well in the game of life. Over the course of time a relationship may need to rekindle passion along the journey to fulfill the inspired vision. There are several factors at play to maintain an active vibrant life to make the vision a reality.

The first factor is to stay abreast of political changes necessary to make adjustments to lifestyle in order to maintain goals in alignment with vision. Surround yourself with allies such as friends, colleagues, and/or community to keep you informed and aware of the economy and legislation changes.

Secondly, improve your quality of life and decision making from the feedback of successful entrepreneurs who have well thought out survival and legacy. A well thought out plan helps to make informed decisions swiftly in the event of circumstances. Keep in mind that a good contingency plan has several options for safety.

Rest and relaxation are important for inspiration to recharge passion for creative energy. An individual's overall health is determined based on how rest and relaxation is considered each day. If the body does not receive the proper nutrients, hydration, and rest each day aging and deterioration depending on the amount of time can become an issue.

Lastly, create or share culture with a community or family of unity. Living by values that are participated on a larger scale boosts the performance of life to share innovations, new ideas, inventions, and much more as one is inspired to serve in the capacity of self-worth and dedication of values.

"Individuals who have attended college have a 13 percent lower risk of divorce. Those with "below average" IQs are 50 percent more likely to be divorced than those with "above average" IQs.

The average age for couples going through their first divorce is 30 years old. 60 percent of all divorces involve individuals aged 25 to 39. Wives are the ones who most often file for divorce at 66 percent on average. That figure has soared to nearly 75 percent in some years. If both you and your partner have had previous marriages, you are 90 percent more likely to get divorced than if this had been the first marriage for both of you. If a person has strong religious beliefs, the risk of divorce is 14 percent less and having no religious affiliation makes you 14 percent more likely to get divorced. If you're an evangelical Christian adult who has been married, there's a 26 percent likelihood that you've been divorced—compared to a 28 percent chance for Catholics and a 38 percent chance for non-Christians."[8]

---

[8]   Wilkinson & Finkbeiner Family Law Attorneys. (2021, January 1). DIVORCE STATISTICS: OVER 115 STUDIES, FACTS AND RATES FOR 2020 Retrieved from https://www.wf-lawyers.com/divorce-statistics-and-facts

Values and Beliefs

Are you content with your values and beliefs? Need no changes, things are just fine the way it is or does your values and beliefs cause you to make changes to your current lifestyle? Should values and beliefs be the core of your decision making. Does growth come from improving values and beliefs for success? Do consider these things as it is vital for the relationship to survive, the closer the values in beliefs the more attraction there is in heart, mind, and soul.

Your IQ increase with the more frequent intellectual conversations you entertain as your brain is stimulated with ideas and heart with emotions you tend to make decisions easily and instantly. Having conversation for why choices were made by core values and beliefs sharpens logic to follow the same roadmap for success.

Next, investing time and doing activities together helps to reinforce the love language of natural attraction. Discussing and sharing what took place in the past, present, and what will in the future helps to strategize your success for happiness. Invest your time early to reap the benefits down the road.

Having a treasure map of memories to relate with your mate's heart is priceless. Remember you are the one who creates your memories based on the things you like to do. So, get on it! Each year create a calendar having some fabulous event to share some wonderful memory. Don't go through a year without having done something romantic, exciting, daring, adventurous, or whatever makes your heart sing for joy!

Lastly, create a lifestyle of flexibility, upholding the greatest respect for ethics and morals. If you want the best relationship, then you have to wear that garment of respect. Honor comes with a price doing the right thing and hold each other accountable. You are entrusted with the wellbeing of the relationship's success; make things happen without being rigid but open to an allowance that warrants great ideas to take place and harmonious energy to flow.

Flexibility and Appreciation

Have you ever heard that flexibility is a sign of mental health or a key for a happy marriage?

According to counselor Marcia Naomi's post on psychcentral, having been married over 30 years states Flexibility is Living with an awareness of the other's wants and needs as well as your own.

However, you cannot get confused about who you are and lose sight of your own needs.

Maturity choses the right battles not to argue but stand firm of things of great significance than that of those insignificant events which are petty.

A roadmap with a two-way street is flexibility, not a rigid roadmap of one street going in one direction.

A great relationship has flexibility and grows in appreciation of one another having these four qualities: Supportive, improvises, praises, and compassionate. A supportive relationship is a good indicator of caring to share resources, time, and effort to accomplish goals in unison. The love language here is an act of service that can motivate the relationship and boost performance in accomplishing goals. Generally, gratitude is the recipient of a supportive relationship which grows in appreciation to remain committed in love.

Praise motivates self-esteem to be confident throughout struggles to achieve what is believed. A relationship of praise charges up the mind and heart to overcome hurdles reaching greater self-consciousness in a more positive state of mind.

Improvising allows creativity and discovery to work out solutions to problems by finding a way out of stagnation. How much you do to reach your goals each week is your efficiency to achieving your vision over a given period of time. How you will your mind and heart to make things happen becomes your success whether resource dependent or not. Improvise your way to make whatever possible to reach your vision as you will stand in awe of the greatness what your relationship has achieved.

Today "job seekers are empowered to seek jobs that are more compatible with their life.

About two-thirds of the workers said they are more productive working outside of a traditional office environment, citing fewer distractions and interruptions, reduced stress from not commuting, and minimal dealings with office politics as their main reasons.

The survey found that flexible-job seekers say work/ life balance and salary are the top two factors when evaluating job prospects. Since 2013, work/life balance (75 percent), spending more time with family (45 percent), saving time (42 percent), and limiting stress from commuting (41 percent) have been the top four reported reasons people seek flexible work.

A majority—78 percent—said that flexible work would allow them to live a healthier life, and 86 percent said they would be less stressed.

"Flexible work arrangements help people do their jobs by reducing various forms of stress, whether it's commuting stress or balancing family obligations," said Chai Feldblum, a partner and director of workplace culture consulting at law firm Morgan Lewis in Washington,

D.C. She is a former commissioner on the U.S. Equal Employment Opportunity Commission and co-director of the Workplace Flexibility 2010 public-policy initiative at Georgetown Law School.

Working remotely full-time is the flexible work option of choice among respondents (76 percent), followed by flexible scheduling (72 percent), part-time scheduling (46 percent) and working remotely part-time (43 percent)."[9]

"If the point is to have flexibility to deal with something that may arise during the workday, then it makes sense that full-time remote work is the most preferable option," Feldblum said. "But a smart and strategic employer would include the requirement that people do come in on specific occasions."

Compassion pays attention to weaknesses as a vital sign of love showing mercy to flaws and mistakes allowing your relationship grow healthy in areas of weakness. Openness to express vulnerabilities is key so that there is no misunderstanding of intentions for greater compassion to reveal the heart's flexibility. I'm sure having these four attributes will promote flexibility and appreciation to work well in your relationship.

- Affirm your value
- Prioritize your needs
- Embrace the awkward
- Challenge your thoughts
- Keep good company
- Step away
- Reflect on the good
- Make time for joy
- Go slow
- Ask for help
- Recommended reading
- Takeaway

---

[9]   Maurer, R. (2019, September 10). Flexible Work Critical to Retention, Survey Finds Retrieved from https://www.shrm.org/ResourcesAndTools/hr-topics/talent-acquisition/Pages/Flexible-Work-Critical-Retention.aspx

Create Your Reality

What may be of benefit to you may not be to another; therefore, chose what reality is suitable for your best interest. Today we will discuss four attributes for creating your reality for what future beholds the desires you place into action. Taking action now places you closer to your reality than wishing for something to take place and not taking action. Let's take a closer look at how you can create your reality now.

If you value your relationship, then it should be easy to give what you want in return. This high-quality nature becomes effortless as it becomes the fabric of the relationship for daily living.

In order to create you need peace and with peace happiness to improve the quality of life you live. Now a healthy couple would naturally do better at peace with happiness than without. Peace and happiness are important to build a future together so make sure this becomes the reality you create for success.

When creating a reality, you ought to plan for a lifetime of vested qualities centered on happiness over the course of time. This is fueled by an abundant energy which manifests itself from meeting each other's needs to energize and/or heal the relationship. Although, maintenance is an awareness to upkeep the relationship for mutual feelings of happiness; you never know what beholds your partner's feelings tomorrow to bring back the performance for a more sustainable and energetic relationship.

If you do not plan wisely how you spend your time in the present, then your future may not be so great depending on the resources you have available. Plan your time now for freedom of time in the future and you will be grateful for time freedom. A relationship not working for freedom of time will eventually burn out in financial distress. Therefore, create the reality that allows you time freedom.

"48 percent of those who marry before the age of 18 are likely to divorce within 10 years, compared to 25 percent of those who marry after the age of 25. 60 percent of couples married between the age of 20 -25 will end in divorce. Those who wait to marry until they are over 25 years old are 24 percent less likely to get divorced."[10]

---

[10]   Wilkinson & Finkbeiner Family Law Attorneys. (2021, January 1). DIVORCE STATISTICS: OVER 115 STUDIES, FACTS AND RATES FOR 2020 Retrieved from https://www.wf-lawyers.com/divorce-statistics-and-facts

Social Life

Every relationship needs a social life as it adds value to give and receive insight. Your social life is an extended relationship that grows from the values of your heart. Growth occurs with engaging communication and actionable support for your endeavors having loyalty and trust. Your social life depends upon your network of friends, associates, colleagues, relatives, or whomever has a ranking of respect for how you desire spend your time whether it be for goals, leisure, or activities of interest. Put together the puzzle pieces that make you complete by creating relationships based on values from your heart.

Choose your way of life for which you desire to uphold honorably like a memorial of remembrance. This becomes your culture created from values of your heart. A collaborative effort to implement values from many cultures for the pursuit of creating your own or live by a traditional culture becomes your style. Culture reflects influences of what's inspired by music, food, dance, arts, language and any other form of guidance that allows you to express your way of life. Create culture from values of your heart.

What is the quality of life you live? The tangible or intangible qualities of life such as educational, financial, intellectual, or emotional should be justified and taken in consideration else your personal and social life impairs your success to failure.

Make room to improve your quality of life by seeking out opportunities that reflect a high standard of accountability for doing your best. The following qualities of life are highly regarded to equip your relationship for a great social life. Generally, anyone possessing traits of emotional, intellectual, and financial stability having morals are strong pillars of supporting your social life. Many factors are influenced by society today, like education and politics; this information changes how we make decisions and view the world. No matter what you do in life don't forget to explore opportunities to improve quality of life!

The average length of a marriage that ends in divorce is 8 years.

"Children with involved fathers have less emotional and behavioral difficulties in adolescence. Teenagers who feel close to their fathers in adolescence go on to have more satisfactory adult marital relationships. Girls who have a strong relationship with their fathers during adolescence showed a lack of psychological distress in adult life."[11]

A relationship without time freedom is limited to how much time can be volunteered or shared with friends and family. A flexibility of time offers memorable moments to form bonds united with those loved or cared for shared experiences. A healthy life explores what makes you happy although there are some hurdles to cross; you engage the ability to engage in leisure, adventures, fun and games, or whatever activity that allows you to live life to the fullest. You have the right to create your social life by planning how to spend more time with friends and family.

---

[11] A Call to Commitment: Fathers' Involvement in Children's Learning, published by the U.S. Department of Education. Updated February 19, 2010.

More Data on the Extent of Fatherlessness

"An estimated 24.7 million children (33%) live absent their biological father."[12]

"Of students in grades 1 through 12, 39 percent (17.7 million) live in homes absent their biological fathers."[13]

"57.6% of black children, 31.2% of Hispanic children, and 20.7% of white children are living absent their biological fathers."[14]

"According to 72.2 % of the U.S. population, fatherlessness is the most significant family or social problem facing America."[15]

---

[12] U.S. Census Bureau, Current Population Survey, "Living Arrangements of Children under 18 Years/1 and Marital Status of Parents by Age, Sex, Race, and Hispanic Origin/2 and Selected Characteristics of the Child for all Children 2010." Table C3. Internet Release Date November, 2010.

[13] Nord, Christine Winquist, and Jerry West. Fathers' and Mothers' Involvement in their Children's Schools by Family Type and Resident Status. Table 1. (NCES 2001-032). Washington, DC: U.S. Dept of Education, National Center of Education Statistics, 2001.

[14] Family Structure and Children's Living Arrangements 2012. Current Population Report. U.S. Census Bureau July 1, 2012.

[15] National Center for Fathering, Fathering in America Poll, January, 1999.

Self-Fulfillment

What is the main obstacle that hinders humanity from achieving self-fulfillment, and how can we ignite a fervent drive for success?

Beware of the moments when humanity's representation of the image of YAH is hindered by malevolence (hostile hatred). The essence of all wickedness is rooted in the fear of not fully embodying YAH's image, leading to the gradual erosion of one's moral core and impeding the genuine realization of an abundant life."

When joy becomes the image of YAH, it serves as the cornerstone for cultivating moral strength, fostering authenticity, and enriching one's life with abundance, thus uplifting humanity's spirit and enhancing one's character.

Fear's Role in Hindering Success:

Fear is a natural emotional and physiological response to a perceived threat or danger. It is an instinctual reaction that readies the body to react to potential harm or stress. When one experiences fear, they may feel anxious, apprehensive, or frightened, and their body may undergo various physical changes such as an increased heart rate, heightened alertness, and the release of stress hormones like adrenaline. Fear can vary in intensity and can be triggered by real or imagined threats, making it a fundamental aspect of human survival and adaptation. Here are the action steps to conquer fear.

Fear often plays a substantial role in thwarting success. It can shackle our potential, cloud our judgment, and paralyze our actions. When fear takes hold, we may find ourselves hesitant to take risks, reluctant to step out of our comfort zone, and anxious about the unknown. These limitations can hinder our progress and limit our achievements. Recognizing and confronting our fears is essential for unlocking our full potential and pursuing success.

Guidance Against Fear:

We are reminded not to fear the world, not to fear that which is beyond our control, and not to fear our circumstances.

Overcoming Fear:

1. Trust in YAH: "Trust in the Lord with all thine heart; and lean not unto thine own understanding. In all thy ways acknowledge him, and he shall direct thy paths." - Proverbs 3:5-6 (KJV)

2. Prayer: "Be careful for nothing, but in everything by prayer and supplication with thanksgiving let your requests be made known unto YAH. And the peace of YAH, which passeth all understanding, shall keep your hearts and minds through Yeshua." - Philippians 4:6-7 (KJV)

3. Casting Your Cares on YAH: "Casting all your care upon him; for he careth for you." - 1 Peter 5:7 (KJV)

4. Avoid Dwelling on Worries: "Therefore I say unto you, Take no thought for your life, what ye shall eat, or what ye shall drink; nor yet for your body, what ye shall put on. Is not the life more than meat, and the body than raiment?" - Matthew 6:25-34 (KJV)

5. Facing Fear with Faith: "Now faith is the substance of things hoped for, the evidence of things not seen." - Hebrews 11:1 (KJV)

Certainly, here's some wise counsel contrasting the role of fear in hindering success with the impact of joy in achieving self-fulfillment:

In these trying times, these truths remain more important than ever. If you desire to make a genuine impact in people's lives, feel free to reach out to find like minds to get started on this important journey.

What, in your opinion, is the remedy for conquering fear?

If your guess was "joy," you are absolutely right! Let's explore the reasons why.

Joy is a profound emotional state that brings forth happiness, contentment, and a sense of well-being. It uplifts the spirit, enhances mental awareness, and fosters a positive outlook on life. The impact of joy on one's mental awareness is remarkable, as it reduces stress, anxiety, and fear, thereby promoting emotional and mental well-being.

Guidance for Increasing Joy:

To experience joy and overcome fear, consider the following guidance:

1. Rejoice in the Lord: "Rejoice in YAH always: and again I say, Rejoice." - Philippians 4:4 (KJV)

2. Count Your Blessings: "This is the day which the Lord hath made; we will rejoice and be glad in it." - Psalm 118:24 (KJV)

3. Choose Gratitude: "In every thing give thanks: for this is the will of YAH in Yeshua concerning you." - 1 Thessalonians 5:18 (KJV)

4. Focus on Positive Thoughts: "Finally, brethren, whatsoever things are true, whatsoever things are honest, whatsoever things are just, whatsoever things are pure, whatsoever things are lovely, whatsoever things are of good report; if there be any virtue, and if there be any praise, think on these things." - Philippians 4:8 (KJV)

5. Serve Others with Joy: "Serve the Most High YAH with gladness: come before his presence with singing." - Psalm 100:2 (KJV)

The Impact of Joy in Achieving Self-Fulfillment:

Embracing joy elevates your mental awareness, dispels fear, and leads to a more fulfilling and peaceful life. It is a powerful force that can strengthen your spirit, nurture your mind, and empower you to face life's challenges with optimism and courage. Joy is a gift that, when cultivated, becomes a source of strength and inspiration.

On the other hand, joy is a catalyst for self-fulfillment. It propels us forward with enthusiasm, infuses our efforts with passion, and imbues our lives with a sense of purpose. When we embrace joy, we are more resilient in the face of challenges, more open to opportunities, and more creative in problem-solving. Joy is not just a fleeting emotion; it is a guiding light that leads us towards self-fulfillment, helping us discover our true purpose and live a life of abundance and contentment.

In the journey towards success and self-fulfillment, acknowledging and transcending fear while nurturing joy is a powerful combination. It enables us to overcome obstacles, seize opportunities, and lead a life that reflects our deepest desires and aspirations. In times of fear and uncertainty, remember that joy is not merely a fleeting emotion but a state of being. By incorporating these principles and scriptural wisdom into your life, you can experience the transformative power of joy, rising above fear and finding enduring happiness.

The Discipline of Success:

With the ability to conquer fear, let us transition towards practicing self-discipline as we strive to achieve our goals for self-fulfillment. Self-discipline is the eternal peace of harmonizing your state of being for what makes you feel good to be happy. The best areas of self-fulfillment for dedication are mentioned in the order of precedence:

First, let's take a look at your commitment to your future. Each partner has their own identity and purpose for fulfilling self-worth and happiness. A desire to become the best allows you to fulfill any void of what success you desire. Allow yourself some flexibility to resync your goals to your commitment and meditate to refresh for clarity.

Life balance
checks priorities

If you have any guilt for not doing something then make that be your priority. You can live a life of complacency or what you desire for your life expectancy. The things that make you the most uncomfortable yet guilty are most likely what you ought to check for priority. The more you prolong the years of your life to change, the less you are esteemed to become your best self. A balanced life places priority on realistic goals that you set for your life expectancy.

What motivates and inspires you to do more in life? Going place of interest to learn Taking time to explore places of relevance to your nature of inspiration becomes motivation for your expression of life.

Seeking to learn more about me

The more time you invest for self-mastery, greater is your advancement to achieving your purpose. Seeking out knowledge for your purpose of identity in alignment with those of relevance before you bring clarity to your past, present, and future.

Organize your mind for more time

Organization allows for diverse perspectives to be shared for day to day in a collaborative effort to improve communication for integration of solutions in everyday problems. Managing yourself to share information in a positive format of supporting the relationship to build trust while planning and structuring meetings for personal and business development.

Work and Play

On par with future goals

There needs to be a plan of action to gain self-mastery over the course of work dedicated. Self-Mastery is the path of faith, learning in patience and seeking the wisdom of guidance to increase knowledge and understanding. The play part is the reward or fruit of your labor. Your happiness over time increases the more you play. Reward yourself with the wonderful activities that fills your heart with gladness that your joy be filled and blessings overtake you to a new world of experience.

Why not have a partner who can appreciate your work and play with? Repeat after me:

"I am happy with life to have a partner at play and work, my work is golden as the sun shines over it continuously as my inheritance."

Music and travel selection

Those who have a theme song recognize the power of creation that aura projects over the presence of work created. Because you are blessed by your work, travel becomes a way for advancement into the many dimensions of life to see the world as it truly is without biased stereotypes. Place an importance on the music and travel arrangements in your life as it tells the story of where you are in life and desire to be.

Physical arts of the body for movement

Physical arts allow circulation of oxygen and energy throughout the body. Exercise allows the mind to break free of stagnation to be more effective than ordinary individual. Creative physical arts express how to free the mind from patterns of blockages as it does tension within the body. Free yourself and release your hidden power.

Getting to know
the Family

A Woman's Male Relatives:
Father, Brother, Grandfather, Uncle

A woman's mentality of safety stems from her father's presence and without she survives to protect herself. If you want to get know a woman, then know the men in her life to confirm what role she will play in your life. Based on her relationships with men within family; determines the level of respect and importance of a man. Knowing this helps to identify how a woman is able to support a man's endeavors to look forward to a great future. A woman's relationship with her father is most important as it is the root quality of her behavior for how she interacts with the men in her life. A woman who copes with her past to recognize the circumstances of those men character flaws of her family; even she fully is equipped to be of great support for a healthy relationship. This woman is not insecure nor lack respect in dealings with men and will not relate from a negative state of consciousness.

More than 20 million children live in a home without the physical presence of a father. Millions more have dads who are physically present, but emotionally absent. If it were classified as a disease, fatherlessness would be an epidemic worthy of attention as a national emergency. The impact of fatherlessness can be seen in our homes, schools, hospitals and prisons cited in the documentary film, Irreplaceable. In short, fatherlessness is associated with almost every societal ill facing our country's children. Homes can be fatherless even when a father is present in the home because there can be psychological issues with the father at play that questions abandonment of a child's identity and self-worth.

A Man's Female Relatives: Mother, Sister, Grandmother, Aunt

Have you wondered about the behavior of a man? Well, a man's heart is influenced greatly by his mother early and strengthened significantly be his father later in life. A mother is first to nurture character traits with quality time as the father grooms him for becoming a man. Depending on the relationships with female relatives of his family determines the safety of the woman he chooses. The type of relationship a mother allows for her son along with other female relatives may be the theme of situations for what can occur in his future. Unless, a man learns from the character flaws of women then is he able to safely secure a healthy relationship.

Two parent home

Values and beliefs should not conflict for children to grow up in a healthy environment without confusion. Children that come from motherless homes have difficulties developing bonds with other adults besides the father. There is an increased level of fear and anxiety that is present with children from motherless homes because they are scared that other adults will also leave. There is a two-fold grieving process for children in motherless homes because the lost relationship is missed and then any hope of a reunion with the mother is then abandoned as well. There is an increased risk of future abuse and abandonment occurring at the hands of children who come from motherless homes.

Homes can be motherless even when a mother is still present in the home because there can be psychological issues with the mother at play that cause the same effects of abandonment as actual abandonment does.

Care to be Affectionate

A person's mental and physical health, affection and care can bring about the right stimuli to keep happy sexual experiences for gratification of his or her partner.

Cuddling and caressing are important ingredients for long-term relationship satisfaction, according to an international study, which queried committed, middle-aged couples from five countries. But contrary to stereotypes, tenderness was more important to the men than to the women. Also contrary to expectations, men were more likely to report being happy in their relationship, while women were more likely to report being satisfied with their sexual relationship.

Concern to be supportive for quality time, without quality time you could experience a rocky relationship.

"The divorce rate among people 50 and older has doubled in the past 20 years, according to research by Bowling Green State University. The divorce rate among couples where one spouse is in jail or prison for one year or more is 80 percent for men and close to 100 percent for women.

60 percent of cohabiting couples will eventually marry. However, living together prior to marriage can increase the chance of getting divorced by as much as 40 percent. If you are a female serial cohabiter – a woman who has lived with more than one partner before your first marriage – then you're 40 percent more likely to get divorced than women who have never done so.

The risk of divorce was said to be almost doubled – 97 percent higher – when the mother went out to work but her husband made a "minimal contribution" to housework and childcare. In 2011, Facebook was cited as a major contributor to 1/3 of divorce petitions examined by one U.K. study. In a study by the University of Rochester, researchers said that watching romantic movies and having a conversation around it helps in lowering the divorce rates from 24 to 11 percent in marriages of three years. Pornography addiction was cited as a factor in 56 percent of divorces according to a recent study."[16]

---

[16] Wilkinson & Finkbeiner Family Law Attorneys. (2021, January 1). DIVORCE STATISTICS: OVER 115 STUDIES, FACTS AND RATES FOR 2020 Retrieved from https://www.wf-lawyers.com/divorce-statistics-and-facts

Cabinet of Friends

Choosing your cabinet of friends should come from supportive qualities and great advice. Such supporters' qualities should be the values that sharpen yours are or very close to yours to ensure your success in areas familiar or unfamiliar. How else can you trust the advice would be well suited for a situation you have not experienced. Unless their values are greater or very close to yours.

Friends of motivation, inspiration, and intellectual conversation are good for enjoyable leisure activities and stimulation of the mind for creative work. If you're seeking to grow with long-term friends then these friends you'd become intrigued by thought provoking questions and ideas, differences of opinion, and depth of knowledge.

Living life without friends in business and/or some professional relationship similar to yours does not develop the skills necessary for success to advance towards the future.

Happy life has activities and hobbies that makes you feel great so finding friends that you can enjoy life in this area helps as a big stress reliever and goal accomplishment. Doing the things you love that gives you the most thrilling life helps you to be successful as you're using your heart more each time you feel good.

Marry what you want to attract in your life. The average length of a marriage that ends in divorce is 8 years.

"If a close friend gets divorced, you are 147% more likely to become divorced[17] and 33% more likely if a friend of a friend is divorced. Studies at the University of California and Brown University cite that when a married person works with someone who is in the process of divorcing, it increases the married person chances of divorce by 75%. These same studies also found that people with divorced sisters or brothers are 22% more likely to get divorced than if siblings are not divorced. In a large-scale Canadian survey, 19 percent of men reported a significant drop in social support post-divorce."

---

[17]   Wilkinson & Finkbeiner Family Law Attorneys. (2021, January 1). DIVORCE STATISTICS: OVER 115 STUDIES, FACTS AND RATES FOR 2020 Retrieved from https://www.wf-lawyers.com/divorce-statistics-and-facts

Engagement

Happy communication is grateful for self-worth as this engagement with your partner exemplifies where you are in your relationship.

Humility of inner peace is a virtue to know what you're doing is good and to hold anyone accountable who disturbs your peace having knowledge of self.

An engagement loving honesty as a standard for correction so that there's no misunderstanding with a mutual agreement other relationship.

An immediate availability to share personal liberty shows the type of engagement of the relationship. How much availability do you have in your relationship?

Reflective listening summarizes what's been said and confirms what's been heard this empathy supports the relationship to ensure there is a mutual agreement without misunderstanding between both partners.

Ask questions or clarify what the one has experienced of the past that may relate to the present behavior experienced. Once an acknowledgment of the existing behavior is confirmed by an individual there has to be a readiness to change if the relationship is to move forward. Use an existing behavior assessment or list of concerns that need to be maintained for change over time. Otherwise, unmanaged behaviors can impede on the progress of a happy relationship. Activities help recognize whether the existing behavior is active, yet increases awareness as to how much effort is made to change. Support tailored to the individual's needs in the form of hugs, kisses, and excitement are great motivators of change.

Intervention
for Supportive
Relationships

Close Relationships

In order to make a relationship close we have to assess the strengths and weaknesses. Wherever the weaknesses are determines the amount of effort needed to strengthen the relationship.

Making no attempts to forewarn your partner results in an unpleasant relationship; which could eventually grow apart. A proactive stance is to watch and warn your partner of any indication which matters to steer the relationship in the wrong direction as the outcome is unfavorable. Listening with empathy is important skill that helps to grow each partner to be more attentive to the needs and values of maintain an intimate relationship.

Navigate life together with your partner and as the more in life you share the closer the relationship becomes to be secure in every way for deeper respect to emerge.

The more things a relationship does together spiritually the deeper the reality you create for what you want out of life. Growing together is the foundation of a relationship but if you grow apart spiritually there will be some areas of obscurity that may be uncertain for how the future is envisioned.

"Women who lost their virginity as a teenager are more than twice as likely to get divorced in the first 5 years of marriage than women who waited until age 18 or older. A 2011 study at the University of Iowa found that for both men and women, the loss of virginity before age 18 was correlated with a greater number of occurrences of divorce within the first 10 years of marriage. When compared to women who began sexual activity in their early 20s, girls who initiated sexual activity at ages 13 or 14 were less than half as likely to be in stable marriages in their 30s. – (in this study a stable marriage was defined as a marriage of over five years)."[18]

---

[18] Wilkinson & Finkbeiner Family Law Attorneys. (2021, January 1). DIVORCE STATISTICS: OVER 115 STUDIES, FACTS AND RATES FOR 2020 Retrieved from https://www.wf-lawyers.com/divorce-statistics-and-facts

Dedication of Commitment

A relationship has purpose for attaining excellence in the quality of life, freedom of choices, and a support system for the vision you desire to live.

A supportive role looks to provide or assist whatever is lacking. Working to improve the quality of life together helps to build legacy and happiness for stability of the home. Create freedom of choices from the value of decisions held by beliefs.

The theme of life is to be dedicated to your commitment as it fulfills your vision. A lifelong journey is not fulfilled if there is no vision to dedicate your work towards.

In the beginning of a relationship there needs to be a common understanding of what loving commitment looks like. Because of much of who You are it's only based on your work they're there also needs to be a dedication of commitment to your relationship. This dedication of commitment it's a sense of pride that seeks to fulfill an agreement to achieve a desirable future envisioned of self. What does a dedication of commitment look like you may ask? Well, it starts with the qualities of a supportive role that seeks to build what quality of life aspired of the future. Through continuous efforts to improve the quality of life overtime, freedom is created from the choices that support the fulfillment of vision.

"Imagine that you've had a heated argument with a co-worker, and you call up your husband or wife to talk about it. Your partner can react in one of two ways.

They can assure you that you were right, your co-worker was wrong and that you have a right to be upset.

Or your partner can encourage you to look at the conflict objectively. They can point out reasons why your co-worker may not be so blameworthy after all.

Which of these responses would you prefer?"[19] Do you want a partner who unconditionally has your back, or one who plays devil's advocate?

Which is better for you in the long run?

---

[19] Daley, B. (2020, January 1). The Conversation: The dark side of supportive relationships. Retrieved from https://theconversation.com/ the-dark-side-of-supportive-relationships-128591

Engaging conversations

A great attraction not only has physical features but also has intellectual features for engaging conversations with a beautiful heart. The more you frequent passionate inspiring topics the closer you move to becoming more of who You are to create the reality for what you see best fit. This type of activity compels you to do something more than to be silent. Engaging conversations improve workflow efficiency, being more productive has a great sense of achievement and boost of morale. Having more time for self-evaluation and to accomplish goals to bring your future closer. The more you are engaged with your partner, you maximize your quality of life by integrating values of honesty for a way of life that shortens time of basic routines to advance future goals. In the end both partners' health is well, the relationship is lovely and lively as there is a gene concern for welfare checkup. Both partners get to play doctor with each other knowing the signs of body language, symptoms of pain and stress, you learn how to body functions and operates because you are responsible for loving yourself. Engaging conversations make a lively relationship for the body to operate lovely for happiness long-term.

"If you're like most people, you probably want a partner who has your back. We all tend to want empathetic partners who understand us, care for our needs and validate our views.

These qualities – which relationship researchers refer to as interpersonal responsiveness – are viewed as a key ingredient in strong relationships. Research has identified links between having a responsive partner and being happy and well adjusted.

But having an empathetic partner isn't always a good thing – especially when it comes to your conflicts with others outside the relationship.

When we get into an argument with someone, we tend to minimize our own contribution to the dispute and overstate what our adversary did wrong. This can make the conflict worse.

After being involved in a dispute, we'll often turn to our partners to vent and seek support.

In our study, we found that empathetic and caring partners were more likely to agree with their loved ones' negative views of their adversary and blame the adversary for the conflict."[20]

Healthy Communication Expresses Feelings

Can a relationship be healthy if there is no way to express your feelings openly? If there is a shutdown of communication, when becomes the question of will you ever get the chance to express yourself? Usually because of frustration the conversation is avoided than to deal with the issue. If done for it a period of time this may be a sign of growing apart. Always present yourself with the best effort to resolve any issue now or later until you become light and heart and mind to do it quickly and easily.

Now the question becomes how can you relate to my situation and vice versa? Unaware of how to communicate properly may hinder the growth of the relationship. Confession and transparency for openness and willingness to change is a made your sign of desirable growth. There has to be an attentive ear to hear being open with a mind and heart to grow together, avoiding the signs of growing apart. Can you listen to comprehended attentively? A major key is to know your partner very well besides observing their actions knowing the intentions of their heart than to speculate assumptions is love.

---

[20] Daley, B. (2020, January 1). The Conversation: The dark side of supportive relationships. Retrieved from https://theconversation.com/the-dark-side-of-supportive-relationships-128591

Speaking truly from honest intentions is a great deal of respect for being involved in a loving committed relationship to create a beautiful future in alignment with your vision "We also found that people whose relationship partners responded this way ended up being far more motivated to avoid their adversaries, tended to view them as bad and immoral, and were less interested in reconciliation. In fact, a full 56% of those who had received this type of empathy reported avoiding their adversaries, which can harm conflict resolution and often involves cutting off the relationship.

On the other hand, among the participants who didn't receive this sort of support from their partners, only 19% reported avoiding their adversaries."[21]

---

[21]   Daley, B. (2020, January 1). The Conversation: The dark side of supportive relationships. Retrieved from https://theconversation.com/the-dark-side-of-supportive-relationships-128591

Counsel Your Union

Throughout your course of your relationship there may be unexpected encounters, events, or moments to suddenly impact life. Depending on the external relationships and events, situations arise from many directions, there are always signs in the beginning. So, ask questions to justify the action of why is this happening and how does it affect what you want to achieve?

If an individual has obstacles of the past that still remain then there becomes a stumbling block for reaching self-fulfillment.

Wise counsel is the insurance of peace. Counsel is the fortitude of your home as it creates a spiritual union for the outcome of marriage. Your divinity has a lot to do with speaking things into existence and being true to what you say and do. A healthy marriage plans judiciously for an inheritance and successor (s) to benefit from the appreciation of values created. The last form of counsel is found within the image of parenting. Providing insight to children that they may know themselves very early in life it's a blessing to keep them from stumbling blocks down the road in their life that can affect their growth in obtaining a future relationship.

"Forty-three percent of children in the United States are being raised without their fathers. When the parents are happily married, the risk of divorce of their children decreases by 14 percent. 90% of divorced mothers have custody of their children. Over 79 percent of custodial mothers receive a child support award, while just under 30 percent of custodial fathers receive one. 65% of divorced mothers receive no child support. Over 46 percent of non-custodial mothers completely default on child support, compared to only 27 percent of non-custodial fathers.

The divorce rate for couples with children is as much as 40 percent lower than for those without children. Half of all children in the United States will witness the ending of a parent's marriage. Of this half, close to 50 percent will also see the breakup of a parent's second marriage. If you have twins or triplets, your marriage is 17 percent more likely to end in divorce than if your children are not multiples. If you have a daughter, you're nearly 5 percent more likely to divorce than if you have a son. When there are as many as three daughters that difference spiked to 10 percent. Fathers are significantly less likely – 3 percent – to be living with their children if they have daughters versus sons. Having a baby before marriage can increase the risk of divorce by 24 percent."[22]

---

[22]   Wilkinson & Finkbeiner Family Law Attorneys. (2021, January 1). DIVORCE STATISTICS: OVER 115 STUDIES, FACTS AND RATES FOR 2020 Retrieved from https://www.wf-lawyers.com/divorce-statistics-and-facts

Arrangement of Marriage

If you happen to find someone you feel is a great life partner worthy of marriage, then consider the process below to anchor your spiritual and physical values for that special union of creating social, financial, and intellectual values.

1. Initial agreement of conditions for an acceptable engagement. Amos 3:3, Matthew 18:19

    Establish mutual terms of loving commitment for strong foundation and future growth of your relationship to thrive such as observance of customs, spiritual principles, advancement of goals, business, intellectual and social groups

2. Values and beliefs are the center of goals to endure by faith. (2 Corinthians 6:14, Hebrews 12:2) Law of Attraction works to gravitate your desire towards the success of what you create with others for productive collaboration.

3. Joining of life by faith to establish family and future goals. (Genesis 24:40) Values and beliefs help to establish how to grow a life of unity having all things in common concerning how you live your way of life.

4. Time Period of Engagement. (Job 7:1) Appointed Time

    The period of engagement gauges whether or not the relationship is suitable to continue as mutually agreed. At the appointed time both partners whether six months or one year in the relationship should have a great understanding of whether it is feasible to remain as partners. A partner's responsibility is to make each other aware of any infringements.

5. Rules of Engagement. (Jeremiah 30:17-22, Hebrews 13:4) Outline expectations for loving commitment having a common understanding of what deal breakers would violate the engagement.

6. Vows of marriage. (Numbers 30, Genesis 34:12, Deuteronomy 23:23)

   If partners honor the rules of engagement throughout the time period engaged, then verbal and/or written promises for creating a family can be constructed with intention to never violate.

7. Witnesses of marriage. (Isaiah 8:1-2, Deuteronomy 19:15)

   A marriage is honorable therefore let each partner bring honorable witnesses two or more who can attest to their vows throughout their marriage.

8. Consummation of marriage. (Genesis 29:30, Genesis 30:4)

   The wedding or feast day that two partners designate before the Most High God with two or more witnesses to be joined in union to solidify their vows by accountability. In case neither partner has understanding of marriage, let an honorable man of the Most High God having understanding provide counsel prior to the day of joining them in union.

9. One report of faith. (Matthew 19:6, Genesis 2:23)

   Both partners become one flesh meaning that their report of salvation is joined as one faith, one baptism, one Most High God in whom homage and reverence is given, the man being the head leads the woman. In a situation where a man is behind the woman spiritually unyoked, then let her be patient for his truth to mature.

Plan your business

What good is a relationship without the planning of business? Is there a no plans for seeking financial and legal protection of business then how will you accomplish your vision? Are there no goals created then how will you budget your resources? If you don't account for what you do then how will you invest your time and money? Goals will be always a work of progress but if you don't forecast your goals how can you expect to make your vision come true? Everything you do has to be event driven based on your goals to make your vision a reality. Having a mentor to show you how to invest your time and money helps you to achieve your goals quickly.

"An annual income of over $50,000 can decrease the risk of divorce by as much as 30% versus those with an income of under $25k. Feeling that one's spouse spent money foolishly increased the likelihood of divorce 45 percent for both men and women. Couples that argue about finances at least once a week are 30 more likely to get divorced. The same study also found that couples with no assets at the beginning of a three-year period are 70 percent more likely to divorce by the end of that period than couples with $10,000 in assets."[23]

---

[23] Wilkinson & Finkbeiner Family Law Attorneys. (2021, January 1). DIVORCE STATISTICS: OVER 115 STUDIES, FACTS AND RATES FOR 2020 Retrieved from https://www.wf-lawyers.com/divorce-statistics-and-facts

Advisors of success

Earlier we discussed counsel your union, now we'll discuss having advisors for the success of your business. Seeking financial and legal protection of your assets it's important as you look to secure your legacy with the proper heirs of succession. Knowledge of financial investments and insurance is important for your financial growth from business and Investments. Besides emergency funds, taking council to perform estate planning ensures your legacy is fulfilled.

"The average total cost of divorce in the United States is $15,000. Families with children that were not poor before the divorce see their income drop as much as 50 percent. Almost 50 percent of the parents with children that are going through a divorce move into poverty after the divorce. 27% of recently divorced women had less than $25,000 in annual household income compared with 17% of recently divorced men. 60% of people under poverty guidelines are divorced women and children.

Most Expensive Celebrity Divorces

Mel and Robyn Gibson – $425 million

Arnold Schwarzenegger and Maria Shriver – $250-$300 million

Michael and Juanita Jordan – $168 million."[24]

---

[24] Wilkinson & Finkbeiner Family Law Attorneys. (2021, January 1). DIVORCE STATISTICS: OVER 115 STUDIES, FACTS AND RATES FOR 2020 Retrieved from https://www.wf-lawyers.com/divorce-statistics-and-facts

How to keep your Partner Interested

How to keep your partner interested

At the beginning chapter of choosing the right relationship, we discuss the responsibility of commitment. Now the question is how do you keep your partner interested? Every relationship requires effort so let's look at the level of effort love takes. In choosing the right relationship there's a natural attraction of selection. What this means that there is a meticulous manner of which decisions are made according to what makes you feel good. As you feel about your partner. The more you do this you have a sense of living with purpose because it fulfills and feels good for each other. Sharing values with one another is a pursuit of happiness that makes you feel good for the appreciation you receive. What you do that feels good naturally brings about a great supportive system of values.

The average length of a marriage that ends in divorce is 8 years.

"If your parents are happily married, your risk of divorce decreases by 14 percent.

A new study entitled "Divorce and Death" shows that broken marriages can kill at the same rate as smoking cigarettes. Indications that the risk of dying is a full 23 percent higher among divorcées than married people. One researcher determined that a single divorce costs state and federal governments about $30,000, based on such things as the higher use of food stamps and public housing as well as increased bankruptcies and juvenile delinquency. The nation's 1.4 million divorces in 2002 are estimated to have cost the taxpayers more than $30 billion. An article in the New York Times stated that of couples who seek marriage counseling – 38 percent end up divorced just two years later. Only around five percent of divorces are decided in the courtroom. This means in 95 percent of divorce cases; the parties and their family law attorneys are able to settle issues amicably or in mediation."[25]

---

[25] Wilkinson & Finkbeiner Family Law Attorneys. (2021, January 1). DIVORCE STATISTICS: OVER 115 STUDIES, FACTS AND RATES FOR 2020 Retrieved from https://www.wf-lawyers.com/divorce-statistics-and-facts

How to love genuinely

Wondering how to love your partner genuinely to keep loving you, then pay close attention.

Always be on guard to protect your love from strangers, extended family, and friends no matter who gets in the way, knowing your partner feelings is important in making your presence known your partner is secured in love and nothing will come between you.

Showing concern for your partner's welfare and health physically and sexually. Enjoyable sex is good when the health and personal matters of life is good and sex always is a relief from things that are not good. Loving your partner genuinely tastes consideration for how you are to grow together to create a lifetime of values. Spending quality time is he active sharing and caring to want to do things together for your pursuit of happiness. Here is a list of qualities you may want in your relationship.

List of Qualities	
Conscious Awareness & Cultural	Honesty & Considerate
Explorer, Adventurer & Traveler	Romance & Mindful
Amend Relationships & Diligence of Perseverance	Passionate Thinkers with Shared Interests
Recreation & Outdoors	Go Getters & Givers
Happiness & Energetic	Peacemaker & Creator
Business & Availability	Physical Workout Activities

Cycles of Life Every Seven Years

Every seven years of our life there is a cycle that renews who we are. Much of what is achieved in life is what we become. Beginning with cultural influences, every seven years take a look at the changes of your culture you embraced overtime. Have you ever asked yourself the question why there is a renewal of vows? Every seven years there is a deeper understanding of the relationship as love is the rededication to your commitment it is also a great accomplishment for reaching the vision. Evaluate this journey of seven years to see what values were upgraded and beliefs changed for the better. This helps to appreciate the circle of life you are in to know that where you're going is bringing you closer to your journey. Remember the times that you've overcome life struggles together to support each other through the times of adversity. Knowing this no one could've done it better?

"If your parents married others after divorcing, you're 91 percent more likely to get divorced. According to Nicholas Wolfinger in "Understanding the Divorce Cycle", the risk of divorce is 50 percent higher when one spouse comes from a divorced home and 200 percent higher when both partners do. In addition, children of divorce are 50 percent more likely to marry another child of divorce. Certain studies have shown that daughters of divorced parents have a 60 percent higher divorce rate in marriages than children of non-divorced parents while sons have a 35 percent higher rate."[26]

---

[26] Wilkinson & Finkbeiner Family Law Attorneys. (2021, January 1). DIVORCE STATISTICS: OVER 115 STUDIES, FACTS AND RATES FOR 2020 Retrieved from https://www.wf-lawyers.com/divorce-statistics-and-facts

Life challenges

There are many unforeseen events that strike suddenly and may come in the form of distress of death, unexpected illnesses, and financial loss. A history of pain resurfaces from the past if not dealt with carefully until know the issue is resolved. When you dwell in fear, anxiety, or hesitation your life path becomes obscure. Instead search out to face your fears to overcome this struggle of adversity. Never run from your problems but make it your strength instead of weakness. A victim of fear is unable to cope with the unknown. Scarcity lacks growth as a stagnant partner may find it difficult to cope with relocation over a great distance to live life to the fullest. All these are life challenges of a relationship that should be discussed prior to the arrival of stormy weather.

Deal Breakers

What are your plans for entering a relationship? Did you not consider the arrangement of your partner for life with exceptions being the violations of your agreement to say we have a deal?

Every individual and relationship is unique, and different factors contribute to the dynamics and quality of a relationship. While it's important to prioritize the needs of both partners and maintain open communication, it's also crucial to approach relationships with flexibility and understanding.

Similar to the upkeep of a vehicle or a home, it is important to consider the maintenance of a relationship, particularly in a partnership. Sustaining a loving commitment and fostering mutual consent are essential for the health and well-being of the relationship. Addictions, negative habits, and a lack of self-control can significantly impact quality of life for both partners. Prioritizing personal growth and individual development is crucial for the success of the partnership.

Another essential quality of maintaining the relationship is to take into account pre-existing conditions that have the potential to cause distress over time if left unaddressed. Unresolved family trauma can often result in unresolved issues and emotional baggage resurfacing in the course of the relationship. One such condition that affects numerous families with abusive backgrounds is Post-Traumatic Stress Syndrome (PTSS).

In every relationship, it is crucial to consider potential red flags and warning signs that may indicate the presence of underlying issues or unresolved trauma. This is particularly important when it comes to addressing Post-Traumatic Stress/Slave Syndrome (PTSS) and its impact on marriages. PTSS recognizes the long-lasting effects of stress or slavery and abuse, which can affect individuals and their relationships across generations. By understanding the key aspects of PTSS, we can better identify and address the circumstances that may lead to marital distress and divorce if left unattended.

Here are some crucial points to consider:

1. **Recognizing Intergenerational Trauma:** PTSS acknowledges that the trauma experienced by enslaved individuals has been passed down through generations. This trauma may manifest in various ways, such as feelings of worthlessness, self-doubt, low self-esteem, and internalized oppression. Understanding these effects can help identify potential challenges within the relationship.

2. **Addressing Cultural Loss and Disconnection:** PTSS recognizes the loss of cultural identity and heritage that occurred during slavery and continues to impact individuals today. This disconnection from one's cultural roots can contribute to relationship difficulties. Acknowledging and valuing cultural differences can help create a supportive environment for healing and understanding.

3. **Combating Internalized Oppression:** PTSS explores how the legacy of stress or slavery has influenced beliefs, attitudes, and behaviors within affected communities. Internalized oppression can lead to self-hatred, self-limiting beliefs, and the perpetuation of oppressive systems within relationships. Challenging and rejecting these negative beliefs can promote healing and empower individuals in their relationships.

4. **Addressing Socioeconomic Impacts**: PTSS recognizes the systemic disadvantages and socioeconomic disparities faced by individuals and communities with a history of slavery or abusive relationships. These factors can affect the dynamics of a relationship and create additional stressors. By understanding these challenges, couples can work together to overcome barriers and seek support in achieving shared goals.

Understanding the consequences of divorce resulting from unaddressed PTSS is crucial. The following are potential outcomes to consider:

1. **Communication Breakdown**: PTSS can disrupt effective communication within a relationship, leading to misunderstandings and disconnection between partners. This breakdown in communication can strain the marriage and contribute to marital distress.

2. **Emotional Distance**: PTSS may cause emotional numbness or detachment, making it difficult for individuals to form and maintain emotional connections. This emotional distance can lead to feelings of loneliness and dissatisfaction within the relationship.

3. **Conflict and Hostility**: Unresolved trauma associated with PTSS can contribute to heightened conflict and hostility within the marriage. These unresolved emotions can trigger defensive behaviors, emotional reactivity, and difficulties in managing anger or frustration, creating a toxic environment.

4. **Parenting Challenges**: PTSS can impact an individual's ability to parent effectively, affecting their parenting style and emotional support for their children. This can negatively influence family dynamics and the well-being of children.

5. **Co-dependency or Enmeshment**: In some cases, PTSS can contribute to unhealthy dependency or enmeshment within the relationship. This dynamic can hinder personal growth and autonomy, leading to an imbalanced relationship.

6. **Loss of Trust and Intimacy**: Unaddressed PTSS can erode trust and intimacy between spouses. It can lead to insecurities, difficulties in building trust, and challenges in establishing healthy emotional and physical intimacy.

It's important to note that the consequences of divorce may vary depending on the specific circumstances and individuals involved. However, seeking therapy and professional intervention to address PTSS can offer an opportunity for healing, improved communication, enhanced emotional connection, and the possibility of rebuilding a healthier and more resilient relationship. By recognizing and addressing the historical trauma and its ongoing effects, individuals and couples can work towards breaking the cycles of oppression and abuse, fostering resilience, and reclaiming their identities.

There are factors that can negatively impact a partnership after marriage and potentially lead to its deterioration include if the following situations occur:

1. **Outside influence from family or friends**: When family members or friends exert excessive influence or interfere in the marital relationship, it can create conflict, undermine trust, and erode the couple's ability to make decisions together. Unwanted interference can lead to tension, resentment, and feelings of being torn between loyalty to one's spouse and loyalty to family or friends.

2. **Family jealousy**: Jealousy or envy from extended family members, such as in-laws, can put a strain on the marital relationship. This can manifest in various ways, including attempts to undermine the couple's unity, comparisons, favoritism, or constant criticism. These dynamics can generate hostility and resentment between partners if not addressed and managed effectively.

3. **Family disrespect**: Disrespectful behavior from family members, directed towards one or both partners, can significantly impact a marriage. Whether it's disrespectful comments, belittling, or dismissive attitudes, such behavior erodes the couple's sense of worth, connection, and mutual respect. It can lead to feelings of frustration, hurt, and a decreased sense of emotional safety within the relationship.

4. **Emotionally controlling or abusive relationships**: When one partner exhibits controlling behavior, emotional abuse, or manipulative tactics, it creates an unhealthy dynamic within the marriage. This can include tactics such as gaslighting, constant criticism, isolation, or exerting power and control over the other partner. Such behaviors can lead to a loss of self-esteem, a sense of powerlessness, and emotional distress, ultimately eroding the love and trust between partners.

5. **Neglecting the emotional needs of the partner**: When partners fail to prioritize each other's emotional well-being and neglect to create a safe space for sharing thoughts, feelings, and vulnerabilities, it can diminish the emotional connection and intimacy in the relationship. Over time, a lack of emotional support and empathy can lead to feelings of loneliness, resentment, and a loss of the sense of love and connection.

It's important to address these factors through open and honest communication, setting healthy boundaries, seeking professional help if needed, and prioritizing the emotional well-being of both partners. Creating a safe and nurturing environment where both partners feel respected, valued, and supported is crucial for the health and longevity of a marriage.

The resilience of marriage is worth noting that relationships evolve over time, and priorities can shift as circumstances change. The arrival of children, for example, can bring about new responsibilities and challenges that require adjustment. It's natural for the dynamic between partners to change during such periods, and it doesn't necessarily mean that love is fading away. It may require conscious effort to nurture the relationship and ensure that the needs of both partners are met.

Different couples have different ways of maintaining their bond and connection. While shared values and activities can contribute to a strong relationship, it's important to recognize that not all couples will have the same beliefs or engage in identical practices. The ultimate human experience and the success of a relationship can be subjective and vary from person to person.

Becoming parents often brings about significant changes in a couple's life, including how couples spend their time together. While it's true that raising children can demand a lot of time and attention, it doesn't necessarily mean there is always less time for each other. The impact on the couple's relationship can vary based on factors such as the support network they have, their individual parenting styles, and how they manage their time and priorities.

Initially, the arrival of a child often requires a considerable amount of time and energy, as newborns require frequent feeding, diaper changes, and round-the-clock care. This can naturally reduce the amount of uninterrupted time a couple has for themselves. Sleep deprivation and adjusting to new routines can also contribute to a temporary shift in the dynamics of the relationship.

Eventually children grow and become more independent, parents usually find more opportunities to spend time together. It may require intentional effort and effective communication to ensure that the relationship remains a priority. This can involve scheduling regular date nights or finding moments throughout the day to connect and engage with each other.

Building a strong support network, such as involving family members, close friends, or hired help, can also provide parents with occasional breaks and opportunities to spend quality time together. Open communication and shared responsibilities between partners can help create a balance between parenting duties and nurturing the couple's relationship.

Ultimately, the impact on a couple's time together after becoming parents depends on various factors and the choices made by the individuals involved. While there may be adjustments and challenges along the way, with proper planning and commitment, couples can still find ways to maintain a healthy and fulfilling relationship while navigating the responsibilities of parenthood.

Therefore, your relationship is making a deal with your partner as long as you live with the intent to honor the loving commitment of mutual consent agreed upon.

When two individuals decide to embark on a journey of living together, fostering a mindset of mutual support becomes crucial. As the saying goes, "two is better than one," and when both partners actively work together and provide assistance, it can alleviate stress within the relationship or marriage and create a more comfortable life for both individuals.

Partnership advice for couples about to embark on marriage:

1. **Prioritize Seriousness**: Nonchalant behavior can be a major issue in a relationship. It's essential that both partners take each other and their words seriously. A lack of seriousness can lead to an imbalance of effort and strain the relationship.

2. **Honesty is Key**: Continuous lying and dishonesty are clear deal breakers. Trust is the foundation of a strong partnership, and when it's eroded by deception, it becomes difficult to fully know and trust your partner.

3. **Avoid Laziness**: Laziness can be a red flag in a relationship. Marrying someone who lacks the drive to improve their career, health, hygiene, and financial situation can lead to frustration and resentment.

4. **Shared Goals Matter**: Make sure you and your partner are aligned in life goals. If your paths diverge significantly in terms of career, location, or parenting aspirations, it could strain your relationship, especially if you value quality time together.

5. **Hygiene Matters**: Personal hygiene is crucial. Being with a partner who neglects cleanliness and expects others to clean up after them can be challenging and feel like taking care of a child.

6. **Financial Responsibility**: Financial irresponsibility can jeopardize your dreams of building a stable future. A partner who squanders money on frivolous things and can't manage finances may hinder your financial goals.

7. **Adaptability and Learning**: A partner who resists adapting to the demands of the relationship and learning to improve it can pose a serious challenge. Relationships require growth and adaptation from both sides.

8. **Acceptance is Key**: One of the biggest deal breakers is a partner who refuses to accept you as you are. If your partner keeps your relationship a secret or is ashamed of you, it raises questions about their commitment and reliability.

9. **Family and Friends**: Sometimes, external factors like family and friends can become sources of tension in a relationship. Be prepared for challenges from these quarters and communicate openly with your partner.

10. **Balanced Selflessness**: A relationship should involve both partners giving and taking. If your partner is consistently selfish, demanding, and lacks consideration for your needs, it may not be a healthy and sustainable relationship.

11. **Confirm Instincts and Intuition**: If you harbor persistent doubts and a nagging sense that this relationship might not be the right fit, it's crucial not to dismiss those feelings when considering significant commitments. Instead, heed your intuition and proceed with caution. Take the time to move at a measured pace, carefully observe your partner's actions and behaviors, and engage in open, honest conversations to address your concerns until you find a sense of peace and clarity.

Bear in mind these signs can potentially jeopardize the health and functionality of your partnership. It's crucial to prioritize open communication, cultivating mutual understanding, and embracing compromise to build a resilient and enduring marriage. Additionally, it's advisable to actively seek these three fundamental qualities in a partner, as they are indispensable for the long-term success of your partnership:

A. **Empower and Uplift**: Be a source of empowerment and motivation for your partner. Focus on highlighting their strengths and avoid negative remarks. Remember, for every negative comment, it takes a multitude of affirmations (like 17:1) to counteract its impact. Believe in yourself and inspire confidence in your partner with words like "you are amazing," "we're in this together," or "I'm here to support you." Daily encouragement and recognizing each other's potential should be a deliberate and consistent effort.

B. **Live by Your Values**: Uphold your principles and live in alignment with your core values and beliefs. A successful partnership thrives when both individuals share a common commitment to personal growth and expansion. Never skip your inner appointments (divine) and stay true to your guiding principles.

C. **Demonstrate Your Presence**: Cultivate the skill of being present in your partnership. Don't hesitate to invest your time and attention in moments that are not solely about you. Your consistent presence reflects your dedication to the principles you've set for your relationship. It's a meaningful way to honor your commitment to each other.

Parental advice regarding having children or not in a marriage:

12. **Align on Parenthood**: One of the most critical decisions in a marriage is whether or not to have children. Before tying the knot, ensure that you and your partner are on the same page regarding this life-altering choice. Discuss your desires, concerns, and expectations openly and honestly.

13. **Communication is Key**: If one partner strongly desires children while the other is opposed, it's essential to have a thorough conversation. Seek compromise if possible, but if the divide is too great, it could lead to bitterness and resentment in the future.

14. **Consider Timing**: Timing matters as well. Some may want to delay parenthood to pursue career or personal goals, while others may wish to start a family right away. Discuss your ideal timelines and find common ground.

15. **Seek Support and Guidance**: If you and your partner are at an impasse regarding the decision to have children, consider seeking professional guidance from a therapist or counselor who specializes in family and relationship issues. They can help facilitate a productive discussion and explore potential compromises.

16. **Be Prepared for Change**: Understand that having or not having children can bring significant changes to your lifestyle, priorities, and responsibilities. Be ready to adapt to these changes as a couple.

17. **Respect Each Other's Choices**: Ultimately, the decision regarding parenthood should be made with mutual respect for each other's feelings and choices. Pressuring a partner into a decision they are not comfortable with can lead to resentment and unhappiness.

Incorporating these considerations into your marriage discussions can help you and your partner make a well-informed decision regarding whether or not to have children and ensure that your marriage is built on a foundation of shared values and understanding.

Evaluating one's personal needs, priorities, and compatibility within the relationship is of utmost importance. If a partner consistently prioritizes others over their spouse and neglects the needs of the relationship, it can strain the bond between them. In such cases, it is essential to address the issues and seek resolution. This may involve seeking guidance from couples therapy or, in more challenging situations, considering separation if the problems cannot be resolved.

Partnership plays a critical role in the success of a marriage. It fosters growth and contributes to a sense of peace within the relationship. Without a strong partnership, a marriage can become unstable and burdensome. It is vital for both partners to communicate effectively and collaborate in order to establish a healthy and prosperous partnership. A lack of partnership within a marriage can lead to frustration, arguments, and other issues that may ultimately result in separation.

Without proper planning, commitment, and the establishment of a strong support network, many marriages fail prematurely. One contributing factor to this is the lack of partnership, where external influences from parents, friends, or children dictate the dynamics of the home, rather than the married couple themselves. Insufficient communication, financial challenges, infidelity, and the negative impact of social media can all become deal breakers that make living together unbearable.

Unfortunately, instead of seeking resolution through marital counseling, many individuals today turn to posting their personal lives on social media. Consequently, every aspect of their marital issues becomes publicized for all to see. People seek answers and solutions to their problems on social media, rather than investing quality time in building connections with their partners. This lack of communication and financial struggles can strain a marriage, leading to disagreements and heightened stress.

Infidelity poses a significant threat to a marriage, as it can erode trust and intimacy. Rebuilding the relationship after infidelity requires addressing emotional trauma, reestablishing trust, and fostering intimacy. Infidelity can also give rise to legal complications, financial difficulties, and social isolation. Seeking help from a therapist or counselor is crucial in these circumstances. Honesty and openness are key to understanding the underlying reasons behind the affair and working towards rebuilding trust and intimacy. If both partners are not willing to engage in this process, it can lead to a permanent breakdown of the relationship. Moreover, if infidelity leads to divorce, it can be emotionally taxing, financially burdensome, and detrimental to the well-being of both individuals involved.

Seeking professional guidance can be a crucial element in maintaining a healthy and thriving relationship. Marital counseling or therapy can provide couples with valuable tools, insights, and strategies to navigate challenges and strengthen their bond. A trained professional can offer a neutral perspective, facilitate effective communication, and guide couples towards resolution and growth.

Additionally, cultivating a mindset of mutual support and partnership is essential for a successful marriage. When both partners actively work together and support each other's needs, it creates a strong foundation for the relationship. This involves being there for each other during difficult times, sharing responsibilities, and making joint decisions that consider the well-being and happiness of both individuals. It requires a willingness to listen, understand, and empathize with each other's perspectives and needs.

It's important to remember that every relationship is unique, and what works for one couple may not work for another. Seeking professional guidance and cultivating a mindset of mutual support and partnership are valuable approaches, but it's also crucial for couples to find their own path and strategies that work best for them. Communication, respect, and a commitment to growth and understanding are vital ingredients in any successful marriage.

By fostering a sense of partnership, couples can build trust, enhance communication, and foster a deeper connection. They become allies and companions on their journey through life, providing emotional support, encouragement, and understanding. This mindset of mutual support and partnership helps couples weather challenges and strengthens the bond between them.

In summary, maintaining a successful relationship involves a commitment of mutual respect, communication, and adapting to changing circumstances. Each individual and relationship is unique, and what works for one couple may not work for another. It's important to approach relationships with understanding, flexibility, and a willingness to work through challenges together.

Have you ever experienced feelings of betrayal, disrespect, or dishonesty in your relationship? Disrespect that aims to embarrass, invalidate, or diminish one's worth goes against the foundation of a loving commitment. What about situations where there is a sense of entitlement and invasion of privacy? Have you ever found yourself being portrayed as a victim based on past information, which is then used to justify unrelated actions or decisions? How does all of this make you feel about continuing the relationship? Are there hesitations about remaining in the relationship, even if it's something you never anticipated, and now your heart and mind must bear the memories of both the good and bad times?

In the beginning of a relationship, things may seem wonderful and positive until you encounter the darker side of a person. If you come across someone who displays a personality where anger leads them to perceive everything from a negative perspective, it can be concerning. In many situations, the more you try to explain or justify yourself, the less credibility you seem to have. These are all signs that can indicate a deal breaker. No one, and I mean no one, should ever have to endure such cruelty in a relationship.

A person who lacks control over their anger becomes a ticking time bomb, ready to explode at any given moment. If someone loses self-control and cannot extinguish the fire of rage when triggered, your safety is at risk. In such cases, it is crucial to get out of that relationship swiftly. It is better to never have gone the distance, but if you find yourself in that situation, you know what you must do now. A person who lacks self-love and patience often struggles to manage their own well-being and becomes argumentative when things don't go as expected, attempting to justify their actions. This type of personality avoids self-reflection but involves others in their issues, withholding information for personal gain or presenting a distorted reality.

There are individuals with self-destructive tendencies, marked by uncontrollable habits and addictions. No matter how much you try to help them, ultimately, it is up to that individual to break free from those destructive patterns. Any relationship entangled with such destructive habits will eventually hinder the pursuit of future happiness and fulfillment. It is important to choose wisely the life you want to live and surround yourself with positive influences. Seek happiness and avoid the trials of sadness, as misery often seeks company. You must decide what you truly desire in life, how to handle challenges and successes, and what constitutes a deal breaker for you. What we have discussed today is just a small sample of what can cause a relationship to fail, serving as deal breakers that signal the need to walk away. Remember, a relationship is a mutual agreement. Do not continue a connection with anyone who violates the terms of that agreement or hinders your vision of a happy future.

When two people decide to live together, they should have a mindset of helping each other in every way possible. As the saying goes, "two is better than one," and when both partners work together and help each other, it can ease some of the stress in the relationship or marriage and make life more comfortable for both partners.

It's crucial for individuals to evaluate their own needs, priorities, and compatibility within a relationship. If a partner consistently prioritizes others over their spouse and neglects the needs of the relationship, it can certainly strain the bond. In such cases, it's important to address the issues and seek resolution, which may involve couples therapy or, in some cases, separation if the challenges cannot be resolved.

Partnership plays a critical role in marriage. It produces growth and adds a sense of peace to the relationship. Without a partnership, the marriage can become unstable and burdensome. It is important for both partners to communicate and work together in order to have a healthy and successful partnership. The lack of partnership in a marriage, it can create frustration, arguments, and other issues that can ultimately lead to separation.

Without proper planning and commitment to build and strong marriage and support network, most Marriages Fail Early, including lack of partnership (outside influence from parents, friends, and child dictates what takes place in the home instead of the married couple). The lack of communication, financial issues, infidelity, social media, and lack of partnership can become a deal breaker if the living together becomes unbearable.

Instead of resolving matters with a marital counselor, many today turn to posting their personal lives on social media. Now everything that happens inside their marital home can be seen and found on social media. People are seeking answers to their questions and solutions to their problems on social media instead of spending quality time with each other. A lack of communication and Financial issues can put a strain on a marriage and lead to disagreements and stress.

Infidelity can ruin a marriage. Couples must work through emotional trauma, rebuild trust, and intimacy. Infidelity can also lead to legal problems, financial difficulties, and social isolation. Seek help from a therapist or counselor. Honesty and openness are key. Understand the reasons for infidelity and work on rebuilding trust and intimacy. Moreover, if both partners are not willing to work on rebuilding trust and intimacy, it can lead to a permanent breakdown of the relationship. Howbeit, if the affair leads to a divorce, it can be costly and time-consuming and can have a negative impact on the mental and emotional well-being of both partners.

Nourishment
of Concern

Civilization Moves Abroad

A monsoon blows from Africa to
Asia Along the two trades routes

We got in the wind
Traveled we from Africa to Asia

Prophets informed us of the union
The past would be reconciled with the present

Senses Confirmed by Emotions

The human being experience is derived from one's feeling of the heart, senses, and intelligence emotionally and intuitively. Together this experience creates the reality of something worth living for in the way of life one views to share.

The feelings are the main focus to know what drives us in this journey of life chosen that we are true to self without the reasoning of other influence. The senses confirm what we know to be true as we are honest with ourselves to be vulnerable in the way we feel at all times. The more situations we take notice of the more we can to cope with unfamiliar situations and the unpleasant. Knowledge of these situations gives insight to what surroundings are viable for our wellbeing, however as a guest it is good to know what attire we must have for a proper response that does not offend yet makes aware the position of stance.

There is a remembrance of the emotional feelings that are of kisses, hugs, touches, and holds. These emotional feelings comfort the soul as vibrant energy when felt as love the heart recognizes from one soul to another healing, relief, and joy that fills up the soul for tranquility and stability of the mind and heart.

Emotionally we communicate with one another to share our thoughts and feelings towards one another without speech. The emotional intelligence is a higher degree of communication that takes place than of oral communication. Using speech, the spirit is in harmony with the soul on the account of another's acknowledgment to transmit and receive information within one's senses.

The testing, debugging, and quality checking of familiar senses is referred to as exercise. Although it sounds technical, frequent exercise of the senses gains power of a quick response towards immediate recognition of one's thoughts and feelings to be known without hesitation. This emotional intelligence can increase around those who are willing to share thoughts and feelings. Also, emotional intelligence is increased in the space of time that one is willing to learn from another in the silence of observation. This space of time cohabited becomes a knowledge base of awareness that senses for detection another's thoughts and feelings. Otherwise, learning without a partner can obscure the observation of situations visited frequently if done with biased input. Therefore, an observer must be honest within self to be vulnerable in the way feeling is higher than intelligence to sense accurately the depiction of the situation. This clarity of truth is divine which uses intelligence lastly to decipher the message observed outside the known reference if applied.

A Lack of Family Knowledge

The young perish from the lack of knowledge not attained before a conscious decision is made. The act of ignorance covets young men the desire to lust for women without the consent her guardian's rights before the commitment of loving kindness is consummated. Fornication is the destroyer of a man's soul that cracks the foundation of his house.

The man is head of the house as the bull is to the oxen and the ram to the sheep. On a pasture, there is one shepherd over the flock that endures suffering of his sheep even if they go astray from the order that unites one-fold. A good shepherd maintains order without the oppression of the flock, but with loving kindness does the flock obey. In cases the sheep chooses to go astray, the situation must be examined to reveal what was lost that caused the departure of heart. Whether the loss of heart was incurred to personal reasons or hurt; the peace of the flock has been broken as tension which could result in strife and a sorrow grieved of departure. However, when there is righteous tension a deeper commitment of loving kindness reaches the heart of sheep and restores one-fold back to its pasture.

Who Loves You

Anyone who knows your weakness and chooses to exploit it for personal gain is dishonest. They will use you as a stepping stone.

Anyone who knows your weakness and chooses to reveal it for edification is honest. They will help you overcome obstacles.

Anyone who takes advantage of another's ignorance for selfish motives will not serve your best interests. They will keep you stagnant and in bondage.

The one who loves you is the one whom you can feel joy without pain and is a delight to be around. This is the flower of life and peace.

The one who loves you is willing to serve you in goodwill to see you happy. Going the extra mile no matter the distance to ensure you have peace within your soul.

The one who loves you will stop you from hurting yourself and others so that you reap the goodness of the land rather than suffer the consequences of bringing evil.

The one who loves you will immediately provide you comfort when your soul is distressed, heart-broken, or vexed.

The one who loves you will not hold your faults against you perpetually, bring forth false accusations, make you the focus of blame, belittle your decisions to undermine the reasoning behind it, scorn your actions, nor interrogate you to make you feel inadequate. However, an unresolved past that has nothing to do with you may be the dukka (emotional attachment) that causes them to take it out on you.

The one who loves you will not override your thoughts in conversation but share thoughts for growth as they listen patiently with intent to hear you. The one who loves you will not jump to conclusions, but wait patiently for the matter to be disclosed; asking questions to ensure that what was mentioned was exactly the point of the message delivered.

Life is about being valued and to have the ability to create values. If one is obligated to do things unwillingly, unhappiness is the bitterness of life. Happiness is the greatest value one can have to achieve the dream. The one who loves you will make sure that you are heard at all times, so that your ideas are always valued. The one who loves you will respect your beliefs and will explore any opportunities of creativity that you may have; provided the nature of energy one brings to your presence. The one who loves you will support and not judge or criticize what you do but strengthen you as one is able in the relationship. The same is able to confide those things that are of distress so that you become your best.

The Establishment of a People

A republic for which it stands is represented by the people and is for the people of that community. An upright community helps to make all accountable for the following statements take precedence. A community cannot be upright when it overlooks moral issues in plain sight.

- Never go the before law against another to resolve conflict so that civil unrest is dissolved in the presence of the community guarding the peace of the land.
- Never scream or yell to slander the character of another; but share everything with respect for other's wellbeing.
- Spend quality time and extend friendships of integrity; never disrespect the opinion of another to end with disgust leaving bitterness behind. Give focus to another to know what's on the heart as you express feelings of peace, confirm within your senses the vibe exhibited to reveal the heart of the matter.
- Avoid friction if your heart lacks understanding to forgive and patience to examine the situation before making a decision so that a grudge is not held against another.
- Separate, if situations arise unrestrained, breaking the peace and quality of nature accustomed for one's social wellbeing.
- Never raise up your hand against another to do them hurt as it remains a scar even a witness against you all your days. Why raise a thought to bring evil against anyone no matter the situation in respect of a grudge? Instead walk peacefully with another that you are not charged of wrongdoing in the presence of those among you.
- Cease to persuade one into believing something that was not agreed with the intent to do so from the beginning or time of consideration to partake freely. An uncomfortable feeling of mistrust or changing of one's character presents a dysfunctional behavior that incriminates the affiliate. No matter the annoyance or distraction, be kind to letting one know how you feel without resentment.

If this trouble ceases not from your presence, draw within your comfort zone a distance of space to quickly identify and respond instantly; so that an intrusion is not made consistently breaking the peace of the ground you walk.

A Salutation
of Peace

Let these final words find give place in your heart that the noble honor of a prince, princess, ambassador, or priest declares you before all to do that which is most upright for conscience sakes. Do not to one what you dislike yourself. Learn to sense what your neighbor feels, so that mistrust is not found. Observe what others do, but stay true to what you do, rather than what you want them to do. If you force the hand of others, down the line your hand will be forced in an uncomprisable way. Whatever mercy you give shall be what you receive. Do not overlook the inequality of others for those that have what they need. Whatever you do to one will be multiplied against you. If you take part in darkness the light of joy will leave you. Having not already experienced darkness, there is a manifold hold of temptation that awaits one who refuses the light revealed as truth.

The honor of life chosen from the foundation of the world is of inheritance. Your birthright of fortune continues from blessings of obedience born of divinity. The choice is yours whether or not you accomplish your destiny as accountability is upheld by the nature of things one entertains. Having an absence of fear and self-seeking pride is the reward of an eternal glory for which innumerable generations shall come to see a wonderful joy that's marvelous to the eyes. This chosen journey of life is the inheritance of a Magnificent Warrior. A majesty of excellence stands before all in honor of the universe bringing into existence the manifestations. Blessed is the name honorable according to deeds worthy of praise to blessing the divinity of the Almighty. Let this name be crowned with a salutation "Live Forever". The grand finale opens an impressive salutation for the welcome of most royal kingdom. A nation whose honor is dominion on earth and praise in the heavens. Selah.

Justified by Faith We Live

Laws of The Covenant

Shout when trumpet sounds and the

walls of the stronghold fall down.

Praise and Obedience releases you from the

captivity of your fathers from whatever

Acts of violence they have done.

A house of bondage was made for a people held

captive from immoral acts or crimes against humanity.

Therefore, acknowledge the Most High God in all your ways

to be counted for righteousness.

You cannot build a kingdom with a pretty fool.

Never compare your ministry or skills with

that of another but complement them.

The Most Holy word is settled in him, therefore glorify him in heaven.

This is my glory that I walk in a garment of

praise continually blessing the Most High God at all times.

Six Works of Faith

1. Seek the Most High God Continually

2. Remember the Covenant of Eternal Life

3. Remember the Most High God's marvelous works and judgments

4. Remember your testimonies, signs and wonders of Almighty Power

5. Declare the Almighty Power & Glory among the nations

6. Glory and Honor is the presence of the Almighty Power along with Strength & Gladness of Heart

> How is the city of praise not left, the city of my
> joy! And it shall be to me a name of joy, a praise
> an honor before all nations of the earth.
>
> Which shall hear all the good that I do unto them
> and they shall fear and tremble for all the goodness
> and for all the prosperity that I procure unto it.
>
> Then will I go unto the altar of the Most High God.
> My exceeding joy, upon the harp will I praise him.

Reward of the Righteous

1. Behold, thy King of Kings cometh

2. Rejoice and be glad no matter what

3. His reward is with him

4. Behold, salvation come

5. Thine kingdom come

6. Zion ruleth with the Most High God

7. Behold, his work before him

8. Sought out the holy people

9. The redeemed of Almighty Power, a city not forsaken.

I. Covenant of Eternal Life (Immortality)

A. Hear, O' YIsra'el: The Most High God our Almighty Power, name is One for all nations.

1. Creator of Heavens & Earth: Genesis 1:1; 2:4; Deuteronomy 4:32-40

2. You are made in the Most High God's image, Be Ye Holy: Gen 1:26; 17:1; Lev 11:44

3. Serve and worship the Most High God faithfully: Gen 24:48; Deut. 6:13; 10:12-20, 13:4; 26:10

4. Fear & Praise the Most High won't lie: Deuteronomy 10:14-21; Gen 22:12; 31:42; Num 23:19

5. I AM; Almighty Power of Abraham, Isaac, & Jacob: Exodus 3:6-10, 13-18, 21-22; Gen 17:1

6. Love the Most High God with all heart, mind, and soul: Deuteronomy 6:4-5; 30:2

7. Almighty Power shall prove your ways to reveal truth: Deuteronomy 30:20; Exodus 20:20-24

8. Obey Almighty Power and live long: Exodus 19:4-6; 23:20-22; Deut. 30:20

9. Almighty Power will bless you: Genesis 22:17-18; 28:3-4; Deuteronomy 30:20

10. Never take the Most High God name in vain (Glorify & Reverence): Ex 20:7; Deut. 5:11; 10:20

11. Swear not falsely nor provoke the Almighty Power: Deut. 6:16; 32:16; Lev 19:12

12. Almighty Power visits the iniquity of the fathers: Ex 20:5; Deut. 5:9; Lev 18:25

13. Almighty Power is merciful and forgives: Ex 34:7; Num 14:18; Gen 33:20

14. Plead for Almighty Power to take away reproach: Ex 10:17; Gen 20:17

15. Almighty Power is the Redeemer of YIsra'el: Ex. 20:2; Deut. 5:6; Ex. 15:11-13; Gen 32:28, 35:10

16. The penalty of death is to blaspheme Almighty Power: Lev. 22:31-33; 24:16

17. Never provoke Almighty Power to jealousy (envy): Exodus 34:14; Deuteronomy 4:24; 6:15

18. Blot out book of life: Deuteronomy 32:30-35

19. Covenant made with Abraham and his seed: Genesis 15:13-21; Deuteronomy 29; 31:24-30

B. Vows of Dedication

1. Pay vow according to age valued of estimation: Leviticus 27:2-8

2. Perform all words spoken from lips: Deuteronomy 23:21-23; Leviticus 5:1, 4-5, Num 30:2

3. Man must not break his vow to fulfill all spoken words before Almighty Power: Numbers 30:1-2

4. A daughter must fulfill her vow once heard by Father w/out cancellation: Numbers 30:3-4

5. Father has authority to disannul daughter of any vows spoken: Numbers 30:5

6. A wife must fulfill her vow once heard by Husband w/out cancellation: Numbers 30:6-7, 10-14

7. Husband has authority to disannul wife of any vows spoken: Numbers 30:8, 12-16

8. A widow or divorced woman's vow shall stand against her to be fulfilled: Numbers 30:9

C. The Nazarite Vow of Dedication

1. Abstain from wine and other fermented drinks: Numbers 6:1-3

2. Abstain from eating anything of the grape vine: Numbers 6:4

3. Use no razor on head until dedication has ended: Numbers 6:5

4. Approach no dead body to defile your head for it is the presence of Almighty Power: Num 6:6-8

5. A soul has guilt once defiled by dead body and must shave head and rededicate: Num 6:9-12

6. Present peace offerings and head of consecration at end of vow to rest: Num 6:13-21

D. Covenant of Creation (Laws of Universe)

1. (1st day) Genesis 1:1-5 (Almighty Power creates light)

2. (2nd day) Genesis 1:6-8 (Almighty Power creates sky)

3. (3rd day) Genesis 1:9-13 (Almighty Power creates trees, grass, every herb of its kind on land from water)

4. (4th day) Genesis 1:14-22 (Almighty Power creates Sun, Moon and Stars in firmament)

   a. Two Great Lights: Sun and Moon: Genesis 1:16

   b. New Year, appointed by the season of spring: Genesis 1:14

   c. New Season, appointed by Sun and Month: Genesis 1:14

   d. New Moon or Month beginning of month (1st Day): Exodus 12:2; Numbers 10:10

   e. Day and Night: Genesis 1:4-5, 18

5. (5th day) Genesis 1:20-23 (Almighty Power creates creature of the sea and foul of the air)

6. (6th day) Genesis 1: 24-31; 2:7, 19-20; 8:17 (Almighty Power creates man, animals, creeping things on land)

7. After the Flood a bow was formed as a token of the Covenant: Genesis 9:8-17

E. Covenant: Prayer, Faith, Testimony, Prophecy, Song

1. Covenant Be Fruitful & Multiply: Genesis 9:1-17; 17:1-24; 35:10-15; Deuteronomy 29:10-29

2. Prayer: Genesis 24:12-27, Genesis 32:9-12; Deuteronomy 25:17-19; 26:15-19

3. Faith: Deuteronomy 4:1-13, 33-40; 6:1-22; 7:9-19; 8:2-11; 11:1-22; Genesis 13:14-17

4. Testimony: Genesis 23; 24:39-52; 28:12-17, 20-22; Exodus 4:10-17, 27-31; 5:1-3; 9:1-5

5. Prophecy: Genesis 37:6-7, 9-11; Exodus 7:1-5, 16-25; Deuteronomy 13:1-5, 18:15-22

6. Song of Moses: Exodus 15:1-21; Num 21:17-18; Deuteronomy 32

7. Be perfect (holy) to walk in the ways of Almighty Power: Deuteronomy 25:15; 28:9

F. Laws of Separation

1. Ye are holy and are severed from other people: Leviticus 19:2; 20:7, 26

2. I will be hallowed among the children of YIsra'el: Leviticus 22:32; Numbers 15:40, Gen 32:32

3. Do not gender beasts to breed or plow with diverse kind: Leviticus 19:19; Deuteronomy 22:10

4. Do not sow mingled seed in field of diverse kind: Leviticus 19:19; Deuteronomy 22:9

5. Do not wear garment of diverse kinds of materials: Deuteronomy 22:11

6. Circumcision: Lev 12:1-5; Gen 12:44-48; 17:7-14, 23-27

II. Tribute of Custom

A. Laws Against Idolatry and Paganism

1. You shall have no other gods before the Most High God

    a. You shall not serve other deities: Exodus 20:3-5; Deuteronomy 7:1-5, 16

    b. You shall not bow down nor worship idols: Exodus 23:24; Deuteronomy 7:2, 25-26

    c. You shall not make covenant, nor marriage with idolators: Exodus 23:32-33; 34:14-17

    d. You shall not conceal an idolator nor lead any astray: Deuteronomy 13:6-18

    e. You shall not sacrifice to idols nor eat and drink: Exodus 22:20; Deuteronomy 32:17, 38

    f. You shall not make no mention of idols: Exodus 23:13

    g. You shall not sacrifice your seed to Molech: Leviticus 18:21

    h. You shall not plant a grove of trees near altar to worship: Deuteronomy 16:21

2. Make no standing images

    a. You shall not make graven or molten image: Ex. 20:4; Deut. 5:8; 27:15

    b. You shall not erect to stand up or bow down to idols: Exodus 34:17; Leviticus 19:4; 26:1

    c. You shall destroy all idolatrous works: Deuteronomy 12:1-3

3. No markings for the dead:

    a. You shall not cut your flesh for the dead: Leviticus 19:4, 27-28; 20:1-5; 26:1

    b. Deuteronomy 8:19; 12:1-31; 13:6-18; 14:1-2; 16:21-22; 17:2-7

B. Laws Against Divinations (Familiar Spirits)

1. Never consult familiar spirits, fortune teller, necromancers: Deuteronomy 18:9-14

2. Never practice to become witch or wizard: Exodus 22:18; Deuteronomy 18:10-12

3. Never commit whoredom with Molech (child sacrifice): Leviticus 20:1-5, 18:21, 24-30

4. Never commit in whoredom to seek after familiar spirits: Leviticus 20:6

5. Never learn the abominations of the nations: Deuteronomy 18-9-14; Leviticus 20:22-27

6. Never use enchantments nor charms to seek familiar spirits: Leviticus 19:26, 31

7. Put away any false prophet who rises up: Deuteronomy 13:1-8, 13-18; Deuteronomy 18:20-22

C. Laws Against Blasphemy Even Heresy

1. Do not take the Most High God's name in vain: Deuteronomy 5:11; 10:20

2. Do not do any presumptuous sin: Exodus 21:14; Numbers 15:30; Deuteronomy 17:12-13

3. Put to death anyone worthy of blasphemy: Leviticus 24:10-16,23

D. Persons Excluded from the Congregation

1. 10th generation Bastard (born of fornication): Deuteronomy 23:2

2. 10th generation Ammonite or Moabite: Deuteronomy 23:3-6

3. 2nd generation Edomite: Deuteronomy 23:7-8

4. 2nd generation Egyptian: Deuteronomy 23:7-8

5. A eunuch (castrated man): Deuteronomy 23:1

III. Moral Welfare

A. Requirements for Benevolence (Good Conduct)

1. Justice & Equality: Do no unrighteousness in judgment

   a. No respect of persons: Leviticus 19:15

2. Wear fringes upon borders of garment as reminder of righteousness

   a. To be done throughout generations: Numbers 15:37-41, Deuteronomy 22:12

B. Duties of Respect and Support (Good Conduct)

1. Manners of Home Training Instilled by Parents

   a. Put to death for smiting (blow hard) or cursing your parent: Exodus 21:15,17

   b. Show reverence to parents or be put to death for cursing them: Leviticus 19:3; 20:8

   c. Honor parents and live long life: Deuteronomy 5:16, Ecclesiasticus 3

   d. Stubborn and rebellious son stoned to death: Deuteronomy 21:18-21

   e. Man is head over family: Genesis 2:22; 3:16; Deuteronomy 1:15

   f. The elder shall serve the younger: Genesis 25:23; Exodus 19:7

C. Requirements for Benevolence (According to Time of Life)

1. Redeem firstborn and protect man child (son)

   a. Sanctify firstborn children and animals: Exodus 13:1-3,

   b. Recall Almighty Power's hand from Egypt redeeming firstborn: Exodus 12-16; 34:20

    c. Redeem firstborn males a month old and upward: Numbers 3:40-51, Deut. 15:19-23

    d. Escape or rescued from bondage: Exodus 1:8-22; 2:2; Numbers 18:14-16

2. Teach children diligently (According to Time of Life)

    a. Teach statutes, judgments, and testimonies of Exodus: Deuteronomy 6:17-25

    b. Teach the fear of Almighty Power and rise up daily to learn: Deuteronomy 4:10; 6:7-9; 11:19

    c. Teach the song of Moses: Deuteronomy 31:19; 32:46

    d. Give thanks after you eaten and rejoice: Deuteronomy 8:10; 12:7

3. Age of Accountability

    a. Age twenty years old and up, shall give an offering to Almighty Power. Exodus 30:14

    b. Each male between 20 to 60 years old will give a certain amount. Leviticus 27:3

    c. A census of men from 20 and up for war: Numbers 1:1-4; 14:29; 26:1-4; 32:11-13

4. Elders, Rulers, Wise and Understanding

    a. Rise up and honor man of grey hairs: Leviticus 19:32, Exodus 22:28

    b. Establish order and government: Deuteronomy 29:9-21, 31:27-29, 32:6-8

    c. Judge Righteously: Leviticus 19:15; Exodus 18:13-26; Deuteronomy 1:13-18; 17:11

    d. Wisdom & Understanding: Deuteronomy 4:5-7, 23:9; 26:16-19, 27:1-10

e. Bind in hand and write laws on heart, mind, and doorpost: Deuteronomy 6:1-9, 13-25

f. Never forsake the commandments even righteousness: Deuteronomy 12:8; 13:18

g. Never diminish nor add to commandments: Deuteronomy 4:2; 5:22; 18:15

h. Forgive anyone who commits sin ignorantly: Leviticus 4:2; 5:1-5; Numbers 15:22-26

i. Put away anyone who commits sin willfully: Numbers 15:29-30; Leviticus 26:14-21

j. Put away false prophets: Deuteronomy 11:16-19; 13:1-5

k. Live separate way of life: Exodus 33:16; Leviticus 20:24; Deuteronomy 13:6-9

l. Vengeance belongs to Almighty Power: Deuteronomy 32:35-36, 42; Leviticus 19:18

m. Put away company of falsehood: 2 Thessalonians 3:14; 2 John 1:10; Galatians 1:6-7

n. Setup order to love truth: 1 Corinthians 11:1-6; 2 Corinthians 11:1-9; Revelation 2:2

5. Widows and Orphans (Fatherless)

a. Never hurt them to make them cry: Exodus 22:22-24

b. Rejoice to give food & clothing: Deuteronomy 10:18, 16:9-15, 26:13

c. Leave food in vineyard: Deuteronomy 23:24-25; 24:19-22

d. Never pervert judgment: Deuteronomy 24:17-21, 27:19

6. The Disabled: Deaf and Blind

a. You shalt not curse the deaf nor put a stumbling block: Leviticus 19:14

    b.   Don't make things difficult for those made with disabilities: Exodus 4:11

    c.   Cursed be he that makes the blind to wander out of the way: Deuteronomy 27:18

7.   The Stranger: One Law for All

    a.   Do not vex or oppress strangers: Exodus 22:21; 23:9; Deuteronomy 10:19; 23:7

    b.   Treat the stranger as though they are native born: Leviticus 19:33-34; 24:22

    c.   Leave gleanings for the poor and stranger: Leviticus 19:9-10; 23:22; 25:35-38

    d.   Love the stranger and leave gleanings behind: Deuteronomy 10:19, 24:19-22

    e.   Charge interest (usury) on money: Deuteronomy 23:19-20

    f.   Forbid uncircumcised from eating Passover: Exodus 12:43-48

    g.   A stranger may keep Passover according to ordinance: Numbers 9:14

    h.   Never eat the sacrifices of a stranger: Numbers 25:1-2; Exodus 22:20

    i.   A stranger may eat anything that dieth of itself: Deuteronomy 14:21; 32:17

8.   The Poor, Brother in Poverty

    a.   Give relief to the poor: Leviticus 19:9-10; 23:22; 25:35-38

    b.   Allow your brethren to dwell with fallen to poverty: Leviticus 25:35-38

    c.   Give gladly to the poor and needy, charity: Deuteronomy 15:7-11

    d.   Greatly bless you for delivering the poor among you: Deuteronomy 15:4

    e.   Take no usury of the poor: Exodus 22:25; Leviticus 25:36

    f.   Do not sleep with a poor man's pledge: Deuteronomy 24:12

9. Neighbors

    a.   Love your neighbor of accountability as yourself: Leviticus 19:18

    b.   Help your neighbor in need: Exodus 23:4-5, Deuteronomy 22:1-4

    c.   Never hate or hold a grudge, charma: Leviticus 19:16-17, 24:19-22; Genesis 31:29

    d.   Cursed be he that smites his neighbor secretly: Deuteronomy 27:24

    e.   Never covet or store for yourself eating of vineyard: Deuteronomy 5:21, 23:24-25

    f.   Never oppress when buying and selling: Leviticus 25:14, 17-18

    g.   Never charge interest on money or withhold pledge: Deuteronomy 23:19-20, 24:10-11

D. Character

1. Moral

    a.   Men of Truth, Fear Almighty Power: Exodus 18:21

    b.   Never covet neighbor's possession: Deut. 5:21, Ex. 20:17

    c.   Never steal, rob, or deal falsely: Exodus 20:15, Leviticus 19:11-13, Deut. 5:19

    d.   Never bear false witness: Exodus 20:16, 23:2; Genesis 21:23; Deuteronomy 5:20

    e.   Never shed innocent blood: Deuteronomy 5:17, 21:1-9, Genesis 4:9-16

    f.   Never reveal secrets, slander, or gossip: Leviticus 19:16, Numbers 14:35-37

g. Confess sin (wrongdoing and shame): Leviticus 5:1-5; 26:40-42; Deut. 32:36

h. Confess trespass to repentance: Leviticus 6:2-5; Numbers 5:6-7, 15:27-31

i. Elder shall serve younger: Genesis 25:21-26

j. Faithful Account of Righteousness: Genesis 30:25-34; 39:3-9, 23; 41:38-46

k. Never provoke the spirit of jealousy: Deuteronomy 32:16-31; Numbers 5:29-30

l. Take no bribes for a gift perverteth the words of the righteous: Exodus 23:8

2. Immoral

a. Learning the abominable acts of nations: Leviticus 18:3, 22-30; 20:22-27

b. Fall away to fulfill the lust for pleasure: Numbers 11:4, 34

c. Murmur, Complain, Blame: Num 11:1, 14:27; Ex 16:7-8, Gen 43:9, 44:10, 32

d. Lawlessness of Sodom & Gomorrah: Genesis 18:20-33

e. Stubborn & Rebellious child, Glutton & Drunkard: Deuteronomy 21:18-23

f. Child sacrifice to Molech (pagan practice): Leviticus 20:1-5

g. Cursing the ruler of any people and condemning their acts of worship: Exodus 22:28

h. Commit willful sin (presumptuous) by force: Deut. 1:43, 17:12-13; Num 15:29-31

E. Treatment of Animals

1. Take Young with Mother: Deuteronomy 22:6-7; Leviticus 22:28

2. Never muzzle a beast while working: Deuteronomy 25:4

3. Restore & Rescue life: Leviticus 24:18, 21-22; Deuteronomy 22:1-4

4. Plow unequally yoked: Deuteronomy 22:10

IV. Mortal Rights and Remedies

A. Restitution for Loss

1. If the thief be found, let him pay double: Exodus 22:7-15

2. Recompense his trespass with the principal thereof, and add unto it the fifth part, and give it unto him against whom he hath trespassed. Numbers 5:5-10

B. Temptation

1. Journey of the Wilderness and The Eating of Manna (40 yrs): Exodus 16

2. War Against Enemies (Amalek): Exodus 17

C. Injuries and Damages

1. Owner's Responsibility of Livestock - Exodus 21:28-36; 22:5-6

2. Make it good if you kill or injure a beast, restore that beast. Leviticus 24:18

D. Masters and Servants

1. Hired Hebrew Servant:

   a. Do not defraud the poor hired of wages: Leviticus 19:13; 25:39-43, 53-55

   b. Do not oppress hired servant: Deuteronomy 24:14

    c. Pay hired servant his hire before sundown: Deuteronomy 24:14-15; Exodus 22:26-27

    d. Hired servant is permitted to eat the produced reaped: Deuteronomy 23:24-25

    e. If a man injures a servant, he shall pay the penalty: Exodus 21:20-21, 26-27

2. Master of Hebrew Servant:

    a. Release Hebrew servant sold after six years: Deuteronomy 15:12-18

    b. Treatment of Hebrew servant's livelihood: Exodus 21:1-11, 20-21

    c. Do not return a Hebrew who escapes his master: Deuteronomy 23:15-16

    d. Do not have sex with bondmaid prepared for marriage: Leviticus 19:20-22

    e. Illegal Tender – put to death a kidnapper of a man to sell for money: Exodus 21:16

3. Redeem Hebrew from Stranger: Leviticus 25:47-55

4. Purchase of Stranger Servant: Leviticus 25:44-46; Genesis 9:25-27

E. Credit, Interest (Usury), Pledge (Loan or Promise to Pay), and Collateral

1. Do not collect usury from the poor: Exodus 22:25-27

2. Do not take your brother's millstone to prepare food for pledge: Deuteronomy 24:6

3. Do not take a poor man's pledge, otherwise wait for delivery: Deuteronomy 24:10-13

4. Do not take widow's clothing to pledge: Deuteronomy 24:17

5. Do not collect usury from your brother: Deuteronomy 23:19-20; 24:6,10-13; Leviticus 25:37

6. Do not collect debt from poor in 7th year: Deuteronomy 15:1-11

7. Do not collect debt from your brother in 7th year: Deuteronomy 15:1-2

8. Collect debt from stranger in 7th year: Deuteronomy 15:1-3

9. Never refrain from lending to the poor in 7th year of release: Deuteronomy 17:7-11

F. Contracts and Agreements

1. Ye shall not swear by my name falsely, neither shalt thou profane the name of thy Almighty Power: Leviticus 19:12

2. If a man vows a vow unto the Almighty Power, or swear an oath to bind his soul with a bond; he shall not break his word, he shall do according to all that proceedeth out of his mouth. Numbers 30:1-16

G. Weights and Measures

1. Never commit fraud in measuring: Leviticus 19:11, 35-37

2. Never try matters with bias or partiality: Deuteronomy 25:13-16

H. Inheritance

1. Right of Firstborn

   a. Deuteronomy 21:15-17

2. Twelve Tribes of YIsra'el

   a. Numbers 33:50-56; 34:16-18

   b. Genesis 49; 48:11-22 49

   c. Deuteronomy 33

3. Levirate Marriage

    a. Deuteronomy 25:5-10

4. Zelophehad's Daughters

    a. Women gain possession of father's inheritance to remain in tribe: Numbers 27:1-11

    b. Instructions for tribal inheritance. 36:1-13

I. Possessions and Property

1. Right of Redemption

    a. Sold Possessions: Leviticus 25:25-28

    b. Sold real estate in the walled city: Leviticus 25:29-30

    c. Sold real estate in country: Leviticus 25:31

2. Sanctify property to be holy unto Almighty Power or sell of possession

    a. Valuation to offer up/exchange clean or unclean beast: Leviticus 27:9-13

    b. Valuation to sanctify house: Leviticus 27:14, 25

    c. Redeem sanctified house: Leviticus 27:15

    d. Valuation to sanctify land: Leviticus 27:16-18, 25

    e. Redeem sanctified land: Leviticus 27:19-21

    f. Valuation of sanctified land purchase: Leviticus 27:22-23, 25

    g. Redeem sanctified land purchased; redeem the tithe: Leviticus 27:24,31

    h. Valuation to sanctify and redeem unclean beast: Leviticus 27:26-27

    i. Whatsoever is devoted to Almighty Power shall not be redeemed unless add: Leviticus 27:28-29

    j. Tithe of the land is holy, belongs to Almighty Power: Leviticus 27:30

3. Land & Cattle

    a. The promise of Abraham, Isaac, & Jacob: Deuteronomy 1:8, 21-25

    b. Destroy images when you dwell in the land: Deuteronomy 7:1-5, 25-27

    c. Teach & learn commandments diligently: Deuteronomy 6:1-9, 13-25

    d. Make no marriages or covenants with other nations: Deuteronomy 7:1-5

    e. Never work the firstling of cattle nor shear firstling of sheep: Deuteronomy 15:19

    f. Never remove your neighbor's landmark: Deuteronomy 19:14; 27:17

    g. Owner put to death after it is testified of ox kill life: Exodus 21:28-29

    h. Meddle not with Esau only buy meat and water: Deuteronomy 2:4-7, 25

    i. The land owned by a man shall not be sold forever: Leviticus 25:13-16, 23

    j. The land owned by Levites shall not be sold forever: Leviticus 25:30-34

V. Marriage, Divorce, and Sexual Relations

A. Sexual Violations

1. Introduction of Forbidden Acts

    a. Invitation to observe Almighty Power's commands: Leviticus 18:1-5

2. A eunuch shall not marry any of YIsra'el: Deuteronomy 23:1

3. 10th gen. bastard (born of fornication) shall not marry any of YIsra'el: Deuteronomy 23:2

4. 10th gen. Ammonite or Moabite shall not marry any of YIsra'el: Deuteronomy 23:3-6

5. 2nd gen. Egyptian or Edomite shall not marry any of YIsra'el: Deuteronomy 22:7-8

6. Adultery

    a. Neighbor's wife is forbidden. Leviticus 18:20

    b. Scourge the man that has sex with unfreed betrothed woman. Leviticus 19:20-22

    c. Both are put to death for adultery Leviticus 20:10

    d. Husband's jealousy presented to priest. Numbers 5:11-31

    e. Do not commit adultery Deuteronomy 5:18; 22:22-24

    f. Marry divorced woman is adultery: Matt 5:27-32; 19:9; Mark 10:11-12; Luke 16:18

7. Prostitution (Tramp)

    a. Do not prostitute your daughter. Leviticus 19:29

    b. Do not cause women to be ritual harlots or pervert men Deuteronomy 23:17-18

8. Whoredom, Whoremonger, Sodomite (Oral/Anal Sex/Homosexual)

    a. Whore: Leviticus 21:7-9, Num 14:33, Deuteronomy 23:17

    b. Play the whore in Father's house before marriage: Deuteronomy 22:13-21

    c. Never bring hire of whore or dog (gigolo) into the house of Almighty Power: Deut. 23:18

9. Violation of Uncleanness

    a. Shall not approach woman in purification (menstrual period): Leviticus 18:19; 20:18

    b. Shall not approach woman in child birth purification: Leviticus 12:2-5

10. Incest

    a. Shall not take Father's wife: Leviticus 20:11; Deuteronomy 22:30; 27:20,23

    b. Shall not take son's wife to uncover nakedness: Leviticus 18:15; 20:12

    c. Shall not take a wife and her daughter: Leviticus 20:14

    d. Shall not take sister to uncover nakedness: Leviticus 20:17, Deuteronomy 27:22

    e. Shall not take aunt to uncover nakedness: Leviticus 20:19

    f. Shall not take uncle's wife to uncover nakedness: Leviticus 20:20

    g. Shall not take brother's wife to uncover nakedness: Leviticus 20:21-23

    h. Shall not uncover the nakedness of relatives near of kin: Leviticus 18:6-18

    i. Conclusion: Leviticus 18:24-30; 20:22-24

11. Homosexual Practices

    a. Man or woman shall not lie with same sex: Leviticus 18:22; 20:13

b. Separation of Sexes by wearing gender specific garments: Deuteronomy 22:5

12. Bestiality

    a. Forbidden intercourse with a beast: Leviticus 18:23; 20:15-16

    b. Penalty for intercourse with beast: Exodus 22:19

B. Sexual Relations

1. Betrothed for Marriage and Defiled Acts

    a. Father presents tokens of virginity for accusation: Deuteronomy 22:13-21

    b. Man found with woman in city with betrothed: Deuteronomy 22:23-24

    c. Man found with woman in field betrothed: Deuteronomy 22:25-27, Leviticus 19:20

    d. Philanderer, sex with engaged partner prior to consummation: Deuteronomy 22:23-24

2. Examples of Concubines: A short-term relationship (1 Kings 8:11:3)

    a. Abraham gave gifts unto the sons of the concubines: Genesis 25:1-7, 1 Chron 1:32

    b. The daughter is a maiden (unmarried) and is a man's concubine: Judges 19:24-25

    c. King David took him more concubines and wives out of Jerusalem: 2 Samuel 5:13; 19:5

    d. King David left ten women, which were concubines: 1 Samuel 15:16,16:21-22; 20:3

C. Marriage Long-term

1. Follow man's lead like unto his nature: Genesis 24:1-8, 37-38

2. Leave mother and father and cleave together becoming one flesh: Genesis 2:21-25

3. Take a wife of your kindred: Genesis 24:38

4. Take a cousin to wife: Genesis 28:2, 9; Deuteronomy 18:2-20

5. Take a maid to conceive seed: Genesis 30:3, 7, 9, 10, 12,18; Exodus 22:16

6. Man humbled virgin pays Father dowry: Exodus 22:16-17; Deuteronomy 22:28-29

7. Avoid prompt marriage covenant with the stranger: Deuteronomy 7:3-4; 25:5; Genesis 28:6

8. Never falsely accuse wife of her virginity to suffer guilt: Deuteronomy 22:13-21

9. Be at home 1 year with new wife, exempt from public affairs and work: Deuteronomy 24:5

10. Take another wife to fulfill her duty of marriage: Exodus 21:10-11; Deuteronomy 21:15-17

11. Do not multiply strange wives to turn his heart from the law: Deuteronomy 17:17

12. Take brother's wife after his decease: Deuteronomy 25:5-6

13. No honor to raise up seed in his brother's house: Deuteronomy 25:7-9

D. Divorce

1. Write a bill of divorce after finding uncleanness of woman: Deuteronomy 24:1

2. Depart out of his house: Deuteronomy 24:2

3. Cannot remarry after she marries another: Deuteronomy 24:3

4. Abomination to remarry the woman once married who lain with another man: Deut. 24:4

VI. Ceremony of Sanctification

A. Special Instructions for Conquest

1. **Planting Trees:** Leviticus 19:23-25

2. **First Fruits:** Deuteronomy 26:1-15

3. **Build A House:** Deuteronomy 22:8

4. **Never sow diverse seed:** Deuteronomy 22:9

5. **Sheepfold:** Numbers 32:16-18

B. Laws Requiring Dedications (Devotions)

1. Devote First Ripe Fruits to Almighty Power: Exodus 23:14-19; Numbers 18:8-14; Leviticus 2:12-14

2. Redeem first born of man and beast: Exodus 22:29-30; 34:19-20

3. Do not redeem if blemish is found of first born: Deuteronomy 15:19-23

C. Laws Requiring First Fruits, Tithing, Free Will Offering, Holy Things

1. **First Fruits:** Deut. 26; 18:1-8; Ex 22:29-30; 23:16-19; 34:26; Num 13:20; Lev 2:11-16; 23:10-14

2. **Tithe of Land:** Numbers 18:19-24; Deuteronomy 12:5-6, 17, 14:22-29; Leviticus 27:30-34

3. **Tithe of Spoil:** (1/10 of all possessions): Genesis 28:10-22; Numbers 31

4. **Tithe of Levites:** Numbers 18:25-32

5. **Freewill:** Ex 25:2; 35:5; Lev 22:18-23; Deut. 12:5-17; 16:10; 23:23; Num 30; Gen 28:20-22

6. Celebrate the feast appointed in its season, rest & refresh: Exodus 23:14-17; 34:23-24

7. Rejoice men to present your offering in the appointed time: Deuteronomy 16:16-17

D. Ordinance of Shabbat (Sabbath)

1. The Seventh Day is Appointed Time for Holy Gathering & Rest

   a. Work shall be done in 6 days: Genesis 2:2-3; Deuteronomy 5:13-15; Leviticus 23:3

   b. Sanctify Shabbat preparation of double portion on 6th day: Exodus 16:5, 23-31

   c. Never make long journey on Sabbath day: Exodus 16:29

   d. Never work on 7th day within your dwelling: Exodus 20:8-12; 23:12; 31:12-17

   e. Rest on 7th day even in earing and harvest time: Exodus 23:12, 34:21

   f. Keep sabbaths to reverence sanctuary: Leviticus 19:3, 30; 23:1-3, 26:2

   g. 7th day is sign of everlasting covenant: Exodus 31:16-17

   h. Blow Trumpet on Shabbat: Numbers 10:10

E. Ordinance of the New Moon (Full Moon)

1. The Beginning of the Month(s) is Appointed Time of Celebration

   a. Full Moon created for the beginning of months: Genesis 1:16-18, 8:13, Exodus 12:2

   b. Moon appointed for seasons: Genesis 1:14-15, 8:22, Psalm 104:19, 74:17

   c. Blow Trumpet in New Moon: Numbers 10:10, Psalm 81:3-5

   d. Hear from Most High at Night to deliver on 1st Day: Numbers 1:1, 18, Deuteronomy 1:3

F. The Salvation Plan (Holy Feast Gatherings)

1. Passover (1st Month, 14th, March-April) The Night children of Israel departed from Egypt

   a. Keep the Passover on 14th day of 1st Month: Leviticus 23:1-5; Numbers 28:16-25

   b. Keep male lamb without blemish from 10th - 14th day: Exodus 12:1-5

   c. Kill and eat the Passover, cover doorpost: Exodus 12:6-13, 21-25; Deut. 16:1-8

   d. Eat Passover with Bitter Herbs, Unleavened Bread: Exodus 12:8, 18, 34

   e. A Memorial forever: Exodus 12:26-42, 51; 13:1-22, 14-16; 14:26-31; Numbers 33:3

   f. Ordinance of Passover - teach children: Exodus 12:43-50; 13:10-15; Genesis 17:10-14

   g. Provision of missing Passover in the 1st Month: Numbers 9:10-14

   h. Never take any of the Passover lamb from place eaten: Exodus 12:46

2. Feast of Unleavened Bread (1st Month, 15th - 21st Day, March-April) Rejoice in Victory!

    a. Worship on 15th day and 21st day of 1st Month: Leviticus 23:5-8

    b. Put away leaven and eat unleavened for 7 days: Exodus 13:3, 6-7; Deut. 16:3, 8

    c. Prepare a feast and do no servile work: Leviticus 23:6-8; Genesis 19:3; Exodus 12:16

    d. Keep the feast for seven days: Exodus 12:14-20,34; 34:18

3. Feast of Weeks (Harvest, First fruits, or Pentecost, May-June) Rejoice in Thanksgiving

    a. Offer first fruits offerings without leaven on 23rd day: Leviticus 23:9-14

    b. Worship on 16th day of 3rd Month (Count 50 days after 22nd day): Leviticus 23:15-16

    c. Offer first fruits offerings with leaven: Leviticus 23:17-22; Numbers 28:26-31

    d. Sanctify yourself for Holy Convocation: Leviticus 23:21; Exodus 19:1-11, 14-16

    e. Keep holy feasts casts out the nations: Exodus 34:22-24; Deuteronomy 16:9-12, 16-17

4. Feast of Trumpets (7th Month, 1st Day, September-October, Rosh Hashanah)

    a. A Memorial of Blowing Trumpets: Leviticus 23:23-25; 25:9; Numbers 29:1-6

    b. Blow Trumpets in Day of Gladness: Numbers 10:1-10; 31:5-6; Exodus 19:13-19

5. Day of Atonement (7th Month, 10th Day, September- October, Yom Kippur)

a. Afflict your souls in the 9th day of the month at even: Leviticus 23:26-32

b. Atonement for sin (sacrifice and scapegoat): Leviticus 16:1-34; Numbers 29:7-11

c. Atonement Money is half (½) shekel for rich and poor: Exodus 30:12-16

6. Feast of Tabernacles (7th Month, 15th-21st Days, September-October, Booths or Ingatherings) Rejoice for the Gathering of Our People in Kingdom

a. Worship on 15th day of 7th Month: Leviticus 23:33-44; Numbers 29:12-40

b. Make boughs of thick trees and rejoice: Leviticus 23:40-43; Genesis 33:17

c. Rest and dwell in booths for 7 days: Leviticus 23:42

d. Rejoice with widows, fatherless, and stranger: Deuteronomy 16:13-17; 31:6, 8-13

e. Three times a year rejoice never appear empty at feast: Exodus 23:15, 17

7. Eighth Day Feast (8th Month, 22nd Day, The Great Day of the Kingdom, End of Ingatherings)

a. Worship on 22nd Day of 7th Month: Leviticus 23:39; Numbers 29:35-39

b. Rest and do no servile work: Leviticus 23:36

G. The Sabbatical Year (7th Year of Release)

1. Six years sow the land but the 7th year you shall let it rest and lie still: Exodus 23:10-11

2. The land shall be meat for you that the poor and the beasts may eat: Leviticus 25:1-7

3. You shall open your hand wide unto thy brother, to thy poor, and to thy needy, in thy land. Deuteronomy 15:1-15

4. Assemble the people to hear the Torah at the close of the 7th year in the feast of tabernacles: Deuteronomy 31:9-13

5. No work done 7th year, sabbatical yr. release from debts and labor: Lev 25:4, Deut. 15:1-2, 12

H. Year of Jubilee

1. Sound the trumpet of the jubilee on the tenth day of the seventh month, in the day of atonement; Count the years of Jubilee by cycles of seven: Leviticus 25:8-13

2. Sell according to the numbers of years left in the jubilee: Leviticus 25:14-16

3. A man shall return to his possession of land in the year of the jubilee: Leviticus 25:23-28,31

4. A man dwelling in a walled city may not redeem after 1 year: Leviticus 25:29-30

5. The Levites dwelling in a city may redeem their possession of land anytime and return to it in jubilee: Leviticus 25:32-33

6. The Levites possession of land in the suburbs may not be sold: Leviticus 25:34

7. The poor shall serve as hired servant unto the jubilee and return to his family: Leviticus 25:39-43

8. If the poor is sold to a stranger then you shall reckon with him that bought him from the year that he was sold to him unto the year of jubilee: Leviticus 25:47-55

VII. Law of Sacrifices & Offerings

A. Holy Things (Sacrifices and Offerings)

1. Rules Pertaining to Offerings

   a. Offer not the sacrifice of Passover with leavened bread: Exodus 23:18; 34:25

   b. Never leave any of the sacrifice of Passover or thanksgiving until the morning: Exodus 12:10; Leviticus 22:29-30

   c. Never break a bone on the sacrifice of Passover: Exodus 12:46, Numbers 9:12

   d. A sacrifice after the 8th day may be accepted and eaten same day: Lev 22:27-30

   e. Offer a male sacrifice without blemish: Deuteronomy 17:1; Leviticus 22:18-24

   f. Never offer up a sacrifice or received bread from a stranger: Leviticus 22:25

   g. Offer up a kid sacrifice on the 8th day after birth without: Leviticus 22:27

   h. Never kill the young and its mother on the same day to offer: Leviticus 22:28-35

   i. Whosoever forsake to keep the Passover shall be cut off: Numbers 9:13

   j. Whosoever forsake to circumcise foreskin of his flesh shall be cut off: Genesis 17:14

   k. Never eat any manner of fat, blood, or that dieth of itself: Leviticus 7:23-27; 17:1-17

   l. Whosoever eats leaven bread from 1st - 7th day shall be cut off: Exodus 12:15, 19

   m. Never eat offering on 3rd day: Leviticus 19:6-8

2. Regulations for Presenting Offerings: Number 4:4-20; 5:9; 18:9, 19, 32

   a. A stranger shall not come near the Holy Things offered: Lev 22:10-15; Num 18:7

   b. Take no produce or livestock till you offer up first fruits: Deut. 26:1-11; 14:22-27; 12:15-25

   c. Take no produce or livestock till you offer tenth to Levites: Num 18:19-24; Lev 27:30-34

   d. If a man redeems his tithes he is to add ⅕ part thereof: Leviticus 27:30-34

   e. Never shall you eat tithes in mourning or for unclean use: Deut. 26:14

   f. The Levites shall offer up tenth of produce or livestock to priests: Num 18:26-32

   g. Never forsake the Levite, fatherless, widow, nor stranger: Deut. 14:28-29; 16:10-11

   h. At the end of the third-year tithe rejoice with gladness: Deut. 26:12-19; 14:28-29

   i. Six years shall you sow thy land and reap harvest: Exodus 23:10-11; Lev 25:1-7

   j. Sow and reap for a cycle of seven sabbaths of years: Lev 25:8-12, 15-22

   k. Proclaim all sacrifices and offerings at the place Almighty Power shall choose: Deut. 12:5-14, 26-28

   l. Never alter the offering or sacrifice except the exchange be holy: Lev 27:9-10

   m. This is the priest due hind cheeks, stomach, and shoulder: Deut. 18:1-3; Lev 10:11-20

   n. The first fruits also is the inheritance of the Levites and priests: Deut. 18:4

3. Burnt Offerings

   a. Leviticus 1:1-17; 6:8-13; 17:8-9 (Instructions for burnt offering/food offering)

   b. Numbers 28:1-8 (Appointed times for burnt offering)

   c. Genesis 8:20, 22:2-13 (Clean animal or human burnt offering command by Almighty Power)

   d. Exodus 27:1 (Dimensions of altar for burnt offering)

   e. Exodus 29:42 (Burnt offering for generations to come)

4. Meat (Grain, Cereal) Offerings

   a. Leviticus 2:1-16; 6:14-23 Never offer with leaven or honey: Leviticus 2:11

   b. Leviticus 2:13 Never offer up offering without salt: Numbers 15:1-21

5. Peace Offerings (Sacrifice of Thanksgiving)

   a. Leviticus 3:1-17; 7:11-21,29-38; 22:21-30

6. Sin Offerings

   a. Leviticus 4:1-35; 5:1-13; 6:24-30 Individual bring forth sin offering, a female kid of goats: Leviticus 4:27-28

   b. Numbers 15:22-31

7. Trespass (Guilt) Offerings

   a. Make restitution for the trespass with a ram, age valued of estimation plus add fifth part thereto: Leviticus 5:14-19; 6:1-7

   b. Process of Trespass Offering: Individual brings forth trespass offering, a female lamb or kid of goats: Leviticus 5:6, 7:1-10, 37, 38

   c. 1st Alternative trespass offering, never cut fowl in half or remove its head: Leviticus 5:7-10

   d. 2nd Alternative trespass offering, never put oil on flour: Leviticus 5:11-13

8. Heave Offerings

    a. The tithes of the children of YIsra'el, which they offer as an heave offering unto Almighty Power: is given as an inheritance to the tribe of Levi: Numbers 18:8-32; Exodus 29:26-28

9. Special Offerings

    a. Sabbath drink, burnt and grain offerings: Numbers 28:9-15

    b. Offering a heifer's neck to atone YIsra'el of unsolved murder: Deuteronomy 21:1-9

B. Order of Rituals

1. Sabbath Day: Leviticus 24:1-9

2. Land Keep Sabbath: Lev 25:1-7, 18-22; Gen 29:27-30, 31:41; Ex 23:10-11

3. Priests shall minister in Sanctuary: Exodus 28:35-43

4. Levites shall minister in any of the gates of YIsra'el: Deuteronomy 18:5-8; Numbers 8:9, 16-26

5. Court of Judgment shall offer up sacrifice if they have erred in ruling: Leviticus 4:13

6. Consecration of Levites: Numbers 8:5-19

7. Feast of Dedication: Numbers 7

8. Feast of Purim: Esther 9:19-22

Which Beasts are designated as 'Clean' and 'Unclean' for Sacrifice to According to OT?

The Old Testament provides specific instruction for how the Most High reveals which animals—including fish and birds—are suitable and unsuitable for human consumption in **Leviticus 11** and **Deuteronomy 14.** Although the lists aren't exhaustive, He reveals guidelines for recognizing animals that are acceptable for food.

The Most High states that **cud-chewing animals with split hooves and cloven foot** can be eaten (Leviticus 11:3; Deuteronomy 14:6). These specifically include the cattle, sheep, goat, deer and gazelle families (Deuteronomy 14:4-5). He also lists such animals as camels, rabbits and pigs as being unclean, or unfit to eat (Leviticus 11:4-8). He later lists such "creeping things" as moles, mice and lizards as unfit to eat (verses 29-31), as well as four-footed animals with paws (cats, dogs, bears, lions, tigers, etc.) as unclean (verse 27).

He tells us that salt and freshwater **fish with fins and scales may be eaten** (verses 9-12), but water creatures without those characteristics (catfish, lobsters, crabs, shrimp, mussels, clams, oysters, squid, octopi, etc.) should not be eaten.

The Most High also lists birds and other flying creatures that are unclean for consumption (verses 13-19). He identifies carrion eaters and birds of prey as unclean, plus ostriches, storks, herons and bats.

Birds such as **chickens, turkeys and pheasants** are not on the unclean list and therefore can be eaten. As it is written in (Luke 2:23-24 & Leviticus 1:14-17) **doves and pigeons** are holy sacrifices acceptable unto The Most High. Yeshua and his disciples never ate anything unclean (Acts 10:14), for he warned us not to sacrifice unto devils.

(1 Corinth 10:19-21) Our bodies are the temple of The Most High for his dwelling. **(2 Corinth 6:14-18)**

Insects, with the exception of **locusts, crickets and grasshoppers,** are listed as unclean (verses 20-23).

Why does The Most High identify some animals as suitable for human consumption and others as unsuitable? The Most High didn't give laws to arbitrarily assert control over people. He gave His laws (including those of which meats are clean or unclean) "that it might be well" with those who seek to obey Him (Deuteronomy 5:29).

Although The Most High did not reveal the specific reasons some animals may be eaten and others must be avoided, we can make generalized conclusions based on the animals included in the two categories.

In listing the animals that should not be eaten, The Most High forbids the consumption of scavengers and carrion eaters, which devour other animals for their food.

Animals such as pigs, bears, vultures and raptors can eat (and thrive) on decaying flesh. Predatory animals such as wolves, lions, leopards and cheetahs most often prey on the weakest (and at times the diseased) in animal herds.

When it comes to sea creatures, bottom dwellers such as lobsters and crabs scavenge for dead animals on the sea floor. Shellfish such as oysters, clams and mussels similarly consume decaying organic matter that sinks to the sea floor, including sewage.

A common denominator of many of the animals The Most High designates as unclean is that they routinely eat flesh that would sicken or kill human beings. When we eat such animals we partake of a food chain that includes things harmful to our bodies. **1 Tim. 4:**[4] For every creature of The Most High is good, and nothing to be refused, if it be received with thanksgiving:[5] **For it is sanctified by the word of The Most High and prayer.**

As nutritionist David Meinz observes: "Could it be that The Most High, in His wisdom, created certain creatures whose sole purpose is to clean up after the others? Their entire 'calling' may be to act exclusively as the sanitation workers of our ecology." (Eating by the Book,1999, p. 225).

In general, we can choose to disregard The Most High's dietary laws written for our salvation and take man's approval of what we should eat and yet be in sin. Yeshua was manifested to take away sin and give life to all who obeys his commandments. **(1 John 3:1-11)**

The following list, based on **Leviticus 11** and **Deuteronomy 14,** identifies many of the animals The Most High designates as clean. The list uses their common names.

CLEAN: BEASTS OF FIELD, FISH OF SEA & FRESH WATERS, LAND & WATER FOWLS

Mammals That Chew the Cud and Part the Hoof	Fish with Fins and Scales		Birds with Clean Characteristics
Antelope	Amberjack	Minnow	Chicken
Bison (buffalo)	Anchovy	Mullet	Dove
Caribou	Angelfish	Perch	Duck
Cattle (beef, veal)	Barracuda	Pike (or pickerel or jack)	Goose
Deer (venison)	Bass	Pollack (or pollock or Boston bluefish)	Grouse
Elk	Black pomfret (or monchong)	Rockfish	Guinea fowl
Gazelle	Blueback	Salmon	Partridge
Giraffe	Bluefish (Snapper blue) Bluegill (Sunfish)	Sardine (or pilchard)	Peafowl
Goat	Bigeyes	SeaBass (Barrimundi)	Pheasant
Hart	Buffalo Fish	SeaTrout	Pigeon
Ibex	Butterfish	Shad	Prairie chicken
Moose	Carp	Silver hake (or whiting)	Ptarmigan
Ox	Cod (Burbot)	Snapper (or ebu, jobfish, lehi, onaga, opakapaka or uku)	Quail
Reindeer	Crappie	Sole	Sagehen
Sheep (lamb, mutton)	Grouper	Steelhead	Sparrow (and other songbirds)
	Grunt	Sucker	Turkey

CLEAN: BEASTS OF FIELD, FISH OF SEA & FRESH WATERS, LAND & WATER FOWLS		
Flounder (Brill)	Tilapia	**Insects**
Haddock	Tarpon	Types of locusts that may include crickets and grasshoppers
Hake	Triggerfish	
Halibut	Trout (or weakfish)	
Herring (or alewife)	Tuna (or ahi, aku, albacore, bonito or tombo)	
Kingfish	Turbot (except European turbot)	
Mackerel (or corbia)	Walleye	
Mahimahi (or dorado, dolphinfish[not to be confused with the mammal dolphin])	Whitefish Whiting	

Clean beast sacrifices are only permitted to be accepted of the Most High God.

- We do not kill the baby with and its mother same day, nor cook it in her milk.
- The clean beasts of the field are of the ox, goat, and sheep family having these requirements:
- Cloven footed, split hoof, and chew the cud (Deuteronomy 14:3-6)
- Any beast that doesn't meet the requirements are forbidden to be sacrificed to the Most High. Ecclesiasticus 45:21

The following list, based on **Leviticus 11** and **Deuteronomy 14**, identifies many of the animals The Most High designates as unclean. The list uses their common ames.

UNCLEAN: BEASTS OF FIELD, CREATURES OF WATERS, FOWLS OF AIR & WATER				
Animals With Unclean Characteristics	Groundhog	Stickleback	Cormorant	Woodpecker
Swine	Hippopo-tamus	Squid	Crane	**Reptiles**
Boar	Kangaroo	Sturgeon (includes most caviar)	Crow	Alligator
Peccary	Llama (alpaca, vicuña)	Swordfish	Cuckoo	Caiman
Pig (hog, bacon, ham, lard, pork, most sausage and pepperoni)	Mole	**Shellfish**	Eagle	Crocodile
Canines	Monkey	Abalone	Flamingo	Lizard
Coyote	Mouse	Clam	Grebe	Snake
Dog	Muskrat	Conch	Grosbeak	Turtle
Fox	Opossum	Crab	Gull	**Amphibians**
Hyena	Porcupine	Crayfish (crawfish, crawdad)	Hawk	Blindworm
Jackal	Rabbit (hare)	Lobster	Heron	Frog
Wolf	Raccoon	Mussel	Kite	Newt
Felines	Rat	Oyster	Lapwing	Salamander
Cat	Rhinoceros	Scallop	Loon	Toad
Cheetah	Skunk	Shrimp (prawn)	Magpie	
Leopard	Slug	**Soft body**	Osprey	
Lion	Snail (escargot)	Cuttlefish	Ostrich	
Panther	Squirrel	Jellyfish	Owl	
Tiger	Wallaby	Limpet	Parrot	

UNCLEAN: BEASTS OF FIELD, CREATURES OF WATERS, FOWLS OF AIR & WATER				
Equines	Weasel	Octopus	Pelican	
Donkey (ass)	Wolverine	Squid (calamari)	Penguin	
Horse	Worm	**Sea mammals**	Plover	
Mule	All insects except some in the locust family	Dolphin	Rail	
Onager	**Marine Animals Without Fins and Scales**	Otter	Raven	
Zebra (quagga)	**Fish**	Porpoise	Roadrunner	
Other	Bullhead	Seal	Sandpiper	
Armadillo	Catfish	Walrus	Seagull	
Badger	Eel	Whale	Stork	
Bat	European Turbot	**Birds of Prey, Scavengers, and Others**	Swallow	
Bear	HardHead	Albatross	Swan	
Beaver	Marlin	Bittern	Swift	
Camel	Monkfish	Buzzard	Teal	
Elephant	Paddlefish	Condor	Vulture	
Gorilla	Shark	Coot	Water hen	

In the King James Version, Leviticus 11:18 and Deuteronomy 14:16 list "swan" as an unclean bird.

VIII. Charge of the Levites for Priestly Service

A. Service of the Levites

1. The Levites shall do the service of the tabernacle instead of all the firstborn among the children of YIsra'el. Numbers 3:39-51; 7:4-9

2. The Levites are given unto the Priests for charge of the congregation: Numbers 3:5-9; 8:5-22

3. The Levites shall wait on the Priest office for service: Numbers 3:10; 8:23-26; 18:1-7

4. The sons of Levi; House of their Fathers: Gershon, and Kohath, and Merari: Numbers 3:17-20

5. The charge of Kohath shall be the ark, table, candlestick, altars, and vessels of the sanctuary: Pitch southward to the tabernacle of the congregation: Numbers 3:27-32; 4:1-15, 17-20; 7:9

6. The charge of Gershon shall be the tabernacle, the tent, the covering thereof, the hanging for the door of the tabernacle of the congregation, the hangings of the court, the curtain for the door of the court, and the cords of it for all the service thereof. Pitch westward of the tabernacle of congregation: Numbers 3:21-26; 4:21-28

7. The charge of Merari shall be the boards of the tabernacle, the bars thereof, the pillars thereof, the sockets thereof, all the vessels thereof, and all that serveth thereto, the pillars of the court round about, and their sockets, and their pins, and their cords. Pitch northward of the tabernacle of congregation: Numbers 3:33-37; 4:29-33

8. The Priests shall pitch eastward of the tabernacle of the congregation: Numbers 3:38; 4:15-16, 28, 33

   v.27 And to the office of Eleazar the son of Aaron the priest pertaineth the oil for the light, and the sweet incense, and the daily meat offering, and the anointing oil, and the oversight of all the tabernacle, and of all that therein is, in the sanctuary, and in the vessels thereof.

v.28 This is the service of the families of the sons of Gershon in the tabernacle of the congregation: and their charge shall be under the hand of Ithamar the son of Aaron the priest.

v.33 This is the service of the families of the sons of Merari, according to all their service, in the tabernacle of the congregation, under the hand of Ithamar the son of Aaron the priest.

IX. Office of the Priests

A. Service of the Priests

1. Defile by dead body: Leviticus 21:1-4

2. Never bald or round corners of head: Leviticus 21:5

3. Never profane (presumptuous sin) the name of Almighty Power, be holy: Leviticus 21:6

4. Never take a profane woman or put away: Leviticus 21:7-8

5. Daughter of priest profane with whoredom: Leviticus 21:9

6. The Priest shall not uncover his head nor rend his clothes: Leviticus 10:3-6, 21:10

7. The Priest shall not drink wine nor strong drink in the tabernacle of congregation: 10:9-11

8. The Priest shall not go near dead: Leviticus 10:1-5; 21:11

9. The Priest shall not profane or depart from the sanctuary: Leviticus 10:7; 21:12

10. The Priest shall marry a virgin: Leviticus 21:13-15

11. The Priest must offer up burnt offering daily each morning and night: Leviticus 6:9-11 (Lev 1)

12. The Priest shall eat meat offering in court of Tabernacle (inner court): Leviticus 6:14-18

13. The Priest shall offer up meat offering burn daily morning and night: Leviticus 6:20-23 (Lev 2)

14. The Priest shall offer up drink offering daily each morning and night: Exodus 29:38-43

15. The Priest shall offer the daily continual burnt, meat, and drink offering: Numbers 28:2-8

16. The Priest shall offer the sabbath continual meat, drink, and burnt offering: Num. 28:9-10

17. The Priest shall offer the monthly meat, drink, and burnt offering: Numbers 28:11-15

18. The Priest shall eat sin offering in court of tabernacle (inner court): Leviticus 6:25-30 (Lev 4)

19. The Priest shall eat trespass offering in court of tabernacle: Leviticus 7:1-7 (Lev 5)

20. Burn remainder of voluntary or sacrifice of peace offering: Lev 7:16-17, 19:5-8, 22:29-31

21. The Priest shall eat the sacrifice of peace offering (outer court): Leviticus 7:29-38 (Lev 3)

22. The Priest shall offer ram of consecration to dedicate upon altar: Exodus 29:15-28

23. The Priest shall eat the ram of consecration at door of Tabernacle: Exodus 29:31-46 (Lev 8)

24. Never approach with issue (blemish): Leviticus 21:17-24, 22:4-9

25. Unclean priest is <u>forbidden to profane (eat) the Holy Things</u>: Leviticus 22:1-4, 14-16

26. Hired Servant bought with money: Leviticus 22:10-11

27. The Priest daughter may not eat after marriage to stranger: Leviticus 22:12-13

28. You are a holy nation, A kingdom of Priests: Exodus 19:6

29. Nation of kings: Genesis 17:5-17; Deuteronomy 14:2; 26:19

30. Never tear High Priest robe, hole in top and middle: Exodus 28:32

31. The High Priest shall bear breastplate of judgment-Urim and the Thummim: Exodus 28:29-30

32. The High Priest shall not enter the sanctuary at all times: Leviticus 16:2, 8:8

33. The Priests shall eat the ram of consecration, sin, trespass, burnt offering: Leviticus 7:37

34. The Priests shall wash hands and feet before they minister: Exodus 30:18-21

B. Tabernacle of the Congregation (Sanctuary)

a. The holy ointment to anoint the tabernacle of the congregation: Ex 30:22-29

b. The holy anointing oil to consecrate the priests: Ex 30:30-31

c. Whosoever compound holy anointing oil upon flesh shall be cut off: Ex 30:32-33

d. Whosoever put perfume upon stranger to smell shall be cut off: Ex 30:34-38

e. You shall keep my sabbaths, and reverence my sanctuary: Leviticus 19:30

ROYAL PRIESTHOOD AFTER ORDER OF MELCHIZEDEK (KINGS & PRIESTS)

SALVATION FROM ZION TO ALL 12 TRIBES AFTER ORDER OF MELCHIZEDEK

COVENANT OF PEACE (Charity, Mercy, Grace)

The law of truth was in his mouth, and iniquity was not found in his lips: he walked with me in peace and equity, and did turn many away from iniquity. (Malachi 2:3-6) Because King David's inheritance is of the kings and priests according to Sirach 45:25 after the order of Melchizedek.

The covenant of David is the inheritance of the kingdom and priesthood.

Sirach 45:25-26. According to the covenant made with David son of Jesse, of the tribe of Judah that the inheritance of the king should be to his posterity alone: so, the inheritance of Aaron should also be unto his seed.

- 26 YAH gives you wisdom in your heart to judge his people... in righteousness, that their good things be not abolished, and that their glory may endure forever.

Hebrews 7:11

- If therefore perfection were by the Levitical priesthood, (for under it the people received the law,) what further need was there that another priest should rise after the order of Melchizedek, and not be called after the order of Aaron?
- For the priesthood being changed, there is made of necessity a change also of the law.

Jeremiah 33:20-21. Thus saith the Most High God; If ye can break my covenant of the day, and my covenant of the night, and that there should not be day and night in their season; Then may also my covenant be broken with David my servant, that he should not have a son to reign upon his throne; and with the Levites the priests, my ministers.

1 Peter 2:4 To whom coming, as unto a living stone, disallowed indeed of men, but chosen of YAH, and precious,

- 5 Ye also, as lively stones, are built up a spiritual house, a holy priesthood, to offer up spiritual sacrifices, acceptable to YAH by Yeshua Ha'Mashiach.
- 6 Wherefore also it is contained in the scripture, Behold, I lay in Sion a chief corner stone, elect, precious: and he that believeth on him shall not be confounded.
- 7 Unto you therefore which believe he is precious: but unto them which be disobedient, the stone which the builders disallowed, the same is made the head of the corner,
- 8 And a stone of stumbling, and a rock of offence, even to them which stumble at the word, being disobedient: whereunto also they were appointed.
- 9 But ye are a chosen generation, a royal priesthood, a holy nation, a peculiar people; that ye should shew forth the praises of him who hath called you out of darkness into his marvelous light;
- 10 Which in time past were not a people, but are now the people of YAH: which had not obtained mercy, but now have obtained mercy.

John 14:27. My peace I give unto you let your heart not be afraid. Romans 8:6 For to be carnally minded is death; but to be spiritually minded is life and peace.

Proverbs 4:23 Keep thy heart with all diligence; for out of it are the issues of life.

Psalms 132:12-18

- [12] If thy children will keep my covenant and my testimony that I shall teach them, their children shall also sit upon thy throne for evermore.
- [13] For the LORD hath chosen Zion; he hath desired it for his habitation.
- [14] This is my rest forever: here will I dwell; for I have desired it.

Hebrews 9:6-11. Now when these things were thus ordained, the priests went always into the first tabernacle, accomplishing the service of YAH… But **Christ being come a high priest of good things to come, by a greater and more perfect tabernacle, not made with hands,** that is to say, not of this building;

Hebrews 10:14-24. For by one offering he hath perfected forever them that are sanctified.

- 15 Whereof the Holy Ghost also is a witness to us: for after that he had said before,
- 16 This is the covenant that I will make with them after those days, saith the Most High God, **I will put my laws into their hearts,** and **in their minds will I write them;**
- 17 And their sins and iniquities will I remember no more.
- 18 Now where remission of these is, there is no more offering for sin.
- 19 Having therefore, brethren, boldness to enter into the holiest by the blood of Yeshua,
- 20 By a new and living way, which he hath consecrated for us, through the veil, that is to say, his flesh;
- 21 And having a high priest over the house of YAH;
- 22 Let us draw near with a true heart in full assurance of faith, having our hearts sprinkled from an evil conscience, and our bodies washed with pure water.

- 23 Let us hold fast the profession of our faith without wavering; (for he is faithful that promised;)
- 24 And let us consider one another to <u>provoke unto love and to good works:</u>

Hebrews 4:14. Seeing then that we have a great high priest, that is passed into the heavens, Yeshua the Son of YAH, let us hold fast our profession.

X. Hygiene Regulations

A. Health Regulations / Cleanliness

1. Leprosy (Plague of mold in skin = Leper)

   a. Leviticus 13:1-59; 14:33-57

   b. Deuteronomy 24:8-9

   c. Numbers 12:10-16

2. Bodily Discharges (Do not approach the unclean nakedness) Leviticus 15:31-33

   a. Man's running issue out of his flesh (sweat, open wound): Leviticus 15:1-7

   b. Man with issue spits upon another: Leviticus 15:8-15

   c. Man's seed of copulation (sperm): Leviticus 15:16-18

   d. Woman's issue of blood (period, menstrual cycle): Leviticus 15:19-30, 18:19; 20:18

   e. Woman's separation of her infirmity (labor of childbirth): Leviticus 12:1-7

B. Purification

1. After Childbirth

   a. A woman after childbirth shall bring forth an offering: Leviticus 12:1-8

2. For Leprosy

    a. Observe the marks of leprosy: Leviticus 14:1-32

    b. Never pluck out marks: Deuteronomy 24:8

    c. Once a leper is cleansed, he shall bring forth an offering: Leviticus 14:10-20

3. For Discharges

    a. Healing takes place within 7 days of cleansing issue: Leviticus 15:13-15, 28-30

4. Concerning Death

    a. Anyone defiled by dead body of any man shall be unclean seven days: Numbers 19:1-22

    b. Defiled by dead body regarding keeping of Passover: Numbers 9:6-7, 10-14

5. Isolation of from Camp (Leprosy, Defiled by Dead body, or Uncleanness at Night)

    a. Separate the children of YIsra'el from their uncleanness Leviticus 15:31

    b. Put them out never defile their camps Numbers 5:1-4; Deuteronomy 23:10-14

    c. The water of separation for a purification for sin Numbers 19:1-10

    d. Whosoever toucheth dead body is defiled for 7 days Numbers 19:11-16

    e. Any soul chooses not to purify is cut off from the congregation Numbers 19:19-22

6. Burial of the Dead

    a. Bury the dead out of your sight not near your dwelling place: Genesis 23:4

C. Hygiene

1. Man's Flesh Defiled

   a. A man who is unclean shall not eat of holy things: Leviticus 7:19, 22:1-10

2. Man's Head / Beard

   a. You shall not round corners of beard: Leviticus 19:27

   b. You shall not make baldness upon your head: Leviticus 21:5

   c. If yellow hair is found, a plague upon the head or beard is unclean: Leviticus 13:29-30

   d. You shall not make baldness upon head: Deuteronomy 14:1

3. Cutting / Marking Body (Tattoo)

   a. You shall not make any imprints in your flesh: Deuteronomy 14:1-2

   b. You shall not cut yourself to grieve: Leviticus 19:28; Deuteronomy 14:1

4. Circumcision of the Covenant even Passover / Castration

   a. Circumcise foreskin of man: Genesis 17:7-14, 23-27; 21:4; 34:13-24; Ex 12:44-45

   b. Childbirth (man child) and Hired Servant: Leviticus 12:1-5; Exodus 4:24-26; 12:44-48

   c. Circumcise Heart: Deuteronomy 10:16; 30:5-7

   d. Never castrate any male species: Deuteronomy 23:1; Leviticus 22:24

5. Decree To Keep Things Separate

   a. Do not mix or pair different animals, seeds or clothing: Leviticus 19:19

   b. Do not wear wool and linen woven together: Deuteronomy 22:11

D. Dietary Regulations (Exodus 23:25)

1. Green Herb (Seed of its Kind)

   a. Eat green herb and fruit with seed: Genesis 1:11-12, 29-30; 2:5-6, 8-9, 15-17

   b. Sow seed and plant trees: Leviticus 11:37; Exodus 10:15

   c. Sow seed in the ground: Deuteronomy 11:10-12; 16:20-21

   d. Do not cross-breed of different species (GMO): Leviticus 19:19

   e. Do not eat fruit of the tree planted in 3rd year: Leviticus 19:23

   f. Fruit is holy to eat in the 4th year: Leviticus 19:24

   g. Never plant diverse seed in vineyard: Deuteronomy 22:9

2. Sanitary Statutes: Blood and Fat of Sacrifices

   a. Never eat or drink blood: Leviticus 7:22-27; 17:10-14; 19:26

   b. Blood is life of flesh: Genesis 9:4; Deuteronomy 12:16, 23-25; 15:23

   c. Never eat the fat of beasts: Leviticus 3:17, 7:22-25

   d. Bring all sacrifices to the door of the tabernacle of the congregation: Leviticus 17:1-9

3. Sanitary Statutes: Set Apart Clean from Unclean

   a. Clean Beast: Leviticus 11:1-3; Deuteronomy 14:1-6; 12:21-22

   b. Clean Fish: Leviticus 11:9; Deuteronomy 14:9

   c. Clean Fowl: Deuteronomy 14:11, 20; Leviticus 5:7; 12:6; Genesis 8:12

   d. Clean Flying Creeping Thing: Leviticus 11:21-22; Deuteronomy 28:38,42

   e. Unclean Beast: Leviticus 11:4-8; Deuteronomy 14:7-8

   f. Unclean Fish: Leviticus 11:10-12; Deuteronomy 14:10

   g. Unclean Fowl: Leviticus 11:13-20; Deuteronomy 14:12-18

h. Unclean Creeping Things: Leviticus 11:23, 29-31, 41-43; Deuteronomy 14:19

i. Cleanliness Law: Your soul is defiled with carcass of unclean beast: Leviticus 11:24-28

j. Cleanliness Law: Your soul is defiled with carcass of creeping thing: Leviticus 11:31-40

k. You are holy and are severed from among other people: Leviticus 11:43-47; 20:25-26

l. A soul unclean eats of sacrifice of peace offering is cut off: Leviticus 7:18-21; 19:5-8

m. Never eat the tendon (hollow) of the thigh for any beast: Genesis 32:24-32

*(The children of YYIsra'el eat not the hollow of Jacob's thigh in the sinew that shrank)

4. Sanitary Statutes: Dead Animals

a. You become defiled with contact of unclean carcass: Leviticus 11:39-40

b. You are holy, eat nothing that dieth of itself: Leviticus 17:15-16; Deuteronomy 14:21

c. You are holy eat nothing torn of beasts: Exodus 22:31; Deuteronomy 12:23

d. Put a difference between clean and unclean: Leviticus 10:10

5. Sanitary Statutes: Never Prepare Young and Mother in Meal

a. Seethe a kid (young) in Mother's Milk: Exodus 23:19, 34:26; Deuteronomy 14:21

b. Never eat egg & hen (mother): Deuteronomy 22:6-7; 14:21

XI. Judicial Legislation of Government

A. Concerning a King

1. Appoint a king from among your brethren: Deuteronomy 17:14-15

2. A king shall not multiply unto himself horses to return to Egypt: Deuteronomy 17:16

3. A king shall not multiply unto himself strange wives to turn his heart: Deuteronomy 17:17

4. A king shall not multiply unto himself silver and gold to turn away: Deuteronomy 17:17

5. A king shall write him a copy of this law in a book: Deuteronomy 17:18

6. A king shall read all the days of his life to learn the fear of Elohim: Deuteronomy 17:19-20

7. Never curse a ruler of any people: Exodus 22:27

B. The Judicial System

1. Establishment of Courts

    a. Judges and officers shalt thou make thee in all thy gates: Deuteronomy 16:18; 17:8-13

    b. Hear the causes between your brethren, judge righteously, and never be afraid of the face of a man nor the honor of the mighty: Deuteronomy 1:15-17; Leviticus 19:15

    c. The cause of both parties shall come before the judges: Exodus 21:22; 22:9

    d. If there is a controversy between men, they shall come unto judgment to make diligent inquisition: Deuteronomy 17:2-13; 19:16-18; 25:1-3

    e. Never curse the ruler of your people: Exodus 22:28

f. Every man shall be put to death for his own sin: Deuteronomy 24:16

g. A man commit a sin worthy of death shall hang him on a tree: Deuteronomy 21:22-23

h. Penalty for intentional or presumptuous sin: Exodus 35:1-3; Numbers 15:32-36

i. One witness shall not testify against any person to cause him to die: Numbers 35:30

j. You shall not falsely testify as a witness: Exodus 23:1-2, 7

k. Take no bribes for a gift perverteth the words of the righteous: Exodus 23:8

l. Never be moved in trying a case based on one's countenance of poverty: Exodus 23:3

m. Never pervert the judgment of the stranger, fatherless, or widow: Deuteronomy 24:17

n. Never pervert the judgment of the poor in his cause: Exodus 23:6

o. Penalty to take bondmaid espoused to husband or Adultery: Leviticus 19:20, 20:10

2. Fairness and Justice

a. Do not pervert the truth to mistreat the poor: Exodus 23:3,6,8

b. Do not deal falsely with neighbor: Leviticus 19:11-15; Deuteronomy 24:17,18

c. Do not wrest judgment on the side of injustice: Deuteronomy 16:19-20; Exodus 23:2

3. Witnesses

a. No false witness: Deuteronomy 5:20, Exodus 23:1,2,7

b. Judgment Needs Two Witnesses: Deuteronomy 17:6-13,19:15-21

4. Punishment (Curses)

    a. Sin worthy of death: Deuteronomy 21:22-23

    b. No man shall be put to death for another's sin: Deuteronomy 24:16

    c. Controversy (Fighting): Deuteronomy 25:1-3

    d. Seed to Molech: Leviticus 20:2-5

C. Crimes Against Humanity

1. Homicide (Murder)

    a. Penalty of Theft: Exodus 21:12-14; 22:2-3

    b. Refuge of Exile for Accidental: Numbers 35:9-15, 22-34, Deuteronomy 19:1-13

    c. Penalty of Death for Intentional: Leviticus 24:17, Numbers 35:16-21, 29-31, 33-34

    d. Judgment of unknown party or cause of murder: Deuteronomy 21:1-9

2. Feticide - Exodus 21:22-25

3. Abduction (Kidnapping)

    a. Illegal Tender – put to death a kidnapper of a man to sell for money: Exodus 21:16

    b. Stealing a man to make merchandise of him or her shall die: Deuteronomy 24:7

4. Mayhem

    a. Exodus 21:26-27

    b. Leviticus 24:19-20

5. Rape - Deuteronomy 22:25-29

6. Assault

   a. If a man smites parents, another man, or servants: Exodus 21:15, 18-21

   b. If a woman wound a man in his secrets: Deuteronomy 25:11-12

D. Crimes Against Property

1. Theft of Personal Property Penalty

   a. Exodus 22:2-3, 7-9

2. Theft of Real Property (cattle)

   a. Exodus 22:1,4

XII. Congregational Council of Assembly

A. Respect for Rulers

1. Do not curse the ruler of the people: Exodus 22:28

2. Discern whether prophet speaks accordingly or falsely: Deuteronomy 18:15-22

3. Do not follow a multitude to do evil: Exodus 23:1-3

4. Establishment for Court of Law

   a. Anyone who is or becomes a warlock: Leviticus 20:6, 27

   b. Blaspheme Almighty Power: Leviticus 24:16

   c. Presumptuous Sin: Numbers 15:30-35, Exodus 31:14, Lev 23:29

   d. Manslaughter (Slayer) and Avenger of Blood: Numbers 35:16-18, 21; Exodus 21:12-14

   e. Eateth or drinketh blood: Leviticus 7:27, 17:10-14

   f. Abomination of nations: Leviticus 18:29, 20:7, 11-15,18; Deut. 12:29, 19:1, Ex 22:19

   g. Approaching Almighty Power's Presence in Uncleanness: Leviticus 22:3, Numbers 19:13-20

   h. False Prophet: Deuteronomy 13:5-9; 18:20-22

5. Overseers: Apostles, Prophets, Preachers/Teachers, Evangelist

   a. Commission of the Apostles: Luke 6:13, Matthew 16:18-19; 10:2; Mark 6:30, Luke 11:49, Acts 1:2; 2:42; 4:33-37; Acts 5:12-29; 8:18; 15:4-33; 16:4; 1 Corinthians 9:2-5; 2 Corinthians 11:5-13; Galatians 2:8

   b. Foundation of the church for perfection of Saints: Ephesians 2:14-21; 3:4-7

    c.   The order and members of the Church office: Ephesians 4:3-13; 1 Corinthians 12:14-31; 1 Thessalonians 2:6; 2 Peter 3:2

6.   The Sanctuary, House of Almighty Power

    a.   Sanctuary at home: Romans 16:1-5, 1 Corinthians 11:19-29, 16:10-20; Colossians 4:10-16; 1 Timothy 3:1-6; Philemon 1:1-9

    b.   Bishop not given to filthy lucre having one wife found blameless: 1Tim. 3:1-7; Titus 1:1-9

    c.   Deacon must not be double tongued ruling house well: 1 Tim. 3:8-13

    d.   Elders as men teach church diligently good doctrine: 1 Tim. 5:1-7,17-25; 1 Peter 5:1-3

    e.   Mothers teach young sisters learn in obedience: 1 Tim. 2:9-13; 5:2-16; 1 Cor 14:34-35

    f.   Women roles in church: Proverbs 31:1-9, Judges 4:1-5, 5:6-7; Joel 2:28-29; Luke 2:36-38; Matthew 8:15; Acts 9:36-40

    g.   Dedicated for church: Romans 16:1-5, 1 Corinthians 11:19-29; 16:10-20, Colossians 4:10-16, 1 Timothy 3:1-6, Philemon 1:1-9

XIII. Rules of Warfare

A. Preparation for Battles

1. Let not your hearts faint, fear not, and do not tremble: Deuteronomy 20:1-9

2. Your eye shall have no pity upon them: Deuteronomy 7:9-24

3. You shall not destroy the fruit trees: Deuteronomy 20:19-20

B. Rules of Siege

1. Proclaim peace to the land you come to fight against: Deuteronomy 20:10-18

2. Never seek nor offer peace to an Ammonite or Moabite: Deuteronomy 23:3-6

3. Blot out the remembrance of Amalek from under heaven: Deuteronomy 25:17-21; Exodus 17

C. Camp Regulations

1. Deuteronomy 23:9-14

D. Soldiers and Marriage

1. Never sell a beautiful woman taken captive in war: Deuteronomy 21:10-14

2. After taken new wife he shall not go to war: Deuteronomy 24:5

3. Go home to dedicate new house: Deuteronomy 20:5

4. Built a battlement (parapet) on rooftop of new house: Deuteronomy 22:8

5. Plant a new vineyard: Deuteronomy 20:6

6. Betrothed to a new wife: Deuteronomy 20:7

7. Fearful and fainthearted: Deuteronomy 20:8

XIV. Charge of Dedication

A. Obedience Required

1. Do not profane my holy name by your actions; but I will be hallowed among the children of YIsra'el: I am the HIGHEST which hallow you. Leviticus 22:31-33

2. What thing soever I command you, observe to do it: thou shalt not add thereto, nor diminish from it. Deuteronomy 12:32

B. Duty to Promulgate (Proclaim or Announce Communication)

1. And it shall be unto you for a fringe, that ye may look upon it, and remember all the commandments of the HIGHEST, and do them; and that ye seek not after your own heart and your own eyes, after which ye use to go a whoring: Numbers 15:37-41

2. At the end of every seven years, in the solemnity of the year of release, in the feast of tabernacles... thou shalt read this law before all YIsra'el in their hearing: Deuteronomy 22:12; 31:9-13

XV. Memorial of YIsra'el

A. Memorial

1. Most High God of Abraham, Most High God of Isaac, and Most High God of Jacob: Exodus 3:15, Psalm 135:13, Genesis 17:9, 21:12; 28:13; Hosea 12:3-6; Exodus 3:15

2. Almighty Power's law may be in thy mouth and deliverance out of house of bondage: Exodus 13:9

3. Keep the Passover, a feast to the Almighty Power throughout your generations: Exodus 12:14

4. Atonement money is to atone for the souls of the Children of YIsra'el: Exodus 30:16, Lev 23:27

5. Bear the names of the Children of YIsra'el before the Most High God: Exodus 28:12, 29

6. These stones shall be for a memorial unto the children of YIsra'el forever: Joshua 4:7

7. Blow trumpets over your sacrifices and offerings: Numbers 10:10 … first day of the month, … a memorial of blowing trumpets… Leviticus 23:24

8. She poured this ointment on my body for my burial: Matthew 26:10-13, Mark 14:9

B. Blessings of Obedience

1. Exodus 15:26; 23:25; Leviticus 26:3-13

2. Numbers 6:22-27; 23:9-24; 24:1-19

3. Deuteronomy 30; 27:1-12; 28:1-14; 11:25-27

4. Genesis 12:1-3; 15:4-7; 22:16-18; 24:58-61; 27:27-29, 39-40; 28:3-4

5. Deliverance from enemies: Exodus 3:21-22; 12:35-36

C. Curses for Disobedience (The Punishments)

1. Chastise 7 times for sins, walking contrary to the covenant: Leviticus 26:14-45

2. All the plagues of bondage shall be upon you 'til you repent: Deuteronomy 28:15-68

3. Levites shall chastise men of YIsra'el loudly: Deuteronomy 27:13-26; 32:20

*Cursed be he that does not confirm all the words of this law to do them. Deuteronomy 27:26

D. Conclusion

1. These are the statutes and judgments and laws, which the HIGHEST made between him and the children of YIsra'el in Mount Sinai by the hand of Moses: Leviticus 26:46, Deut. 5:22, John 5:46

2. If ye keep my commandments, ye shall abide in my love; even as I have kept my Father's commandments, and abide in his love. John 15:10, John 14:15-21, 1 John 5:1-3

3. Let us hear the conclusion of the whole matter: Fear YAH, and keep his commandments: for this is the whole duty of man. Ecclesiastes 12:13

Index/Reference

Academy of Family Mediators (2020, January 1). Prevalence and Effects Retrieved from https://www.mediate.com/divorce/pg60.cfm

Hill, Napoleon. The Law of Success Author. The RALSTON UNIVERSITY PRESS MERIDEN, CONN., 1928 <pgs.28-39> https://www.healthline.com/health/how-to-stop-being-insecure#embrace-the-awkward

Davis, Ben. What are the four areas of self-esteem? https://www.mvorganizing.org/what-are-four-areas-of-self-esteem/ Accessed 2020 <pgs.39-85>

Pietrangelo, Ann. What IQ Measurements Indicate — and What They Don't, https://www.healthline.com/health/what-is-considered-a-high-iq#whats-a-high-iq Accessed 2020 <pgs.74-143>

Goldberg Jones - Divorce For Men. Divorce Statistics: From The Interesting To The Surprising, https://www.goldbergjones-or.com/divorce/interesting-divorce-statistics/ Accessed 2020 <pgs.75-119>

Wilkinson & Finkbeiner, LLP. Divorce Statistics and Facts, https://www.wf-lawyers.com/divorce-statistics-and-facts/ Accessed 2020 <pgs.75 - 132>

Cottrill, Jeffrey. Divorce Magazine, https://www.divorcemag.com/articles/us-military-divorce-rate-rises-again-says-pentagon Accessed 2021 <pg.76>

Scott Ph.D., Elizabeth. How to Improve Your Quality Life, https://www.verywellmind.com/how-to-maintain-a-high-quality-of-life-3144723 Accessed 2020 <pgs.77-113>

Kanaat, Robert. 25 Habits for Improving the Quality of your Life, https://www.wanderlustworker.com/25-habits-for-improving-the-quality-of-your-life/ Accessed 2020 <pgs.77-113>

Tank, Aytekin. 9 Positive Affirmations to Boost Your Work Morale, https://www.lifehack.org/876965/positive-affirmations-for-work Accessed 2020 <pg.79>

Couple Family Psychol. Reasons for Divorce and Recollections of Premarital Intervention: Implications for Improving Relationship Education, https://www.ncbi.nlm.nih.gov/pmc/articles/PMC4012696/ Accessed 2020 <pgs.80-128>

Maurer, Roy. Flexible Work Critical to Retention, Survey Finds, https://www.shrm.org/resourcesandtools/hr-topics/talent-acquisition/pages/flexible-work-critical-retention.aspx Accessed 2020 <pg.86>

The Conversation. IQ tests can't measure it, but 'cognitive flexibility' is key to learning and creativity, https://theconversation.com/iq-tests-cant-measure-it-but-cognitive-flexibility-is-key-to-learning-and-creativity-163284 Accessed 2020 <pgs.84-87>

Eltringham, Mark. Only 7 percent of workers say they're most productive working in an office https://workplaceinsight.net/seven-percent-workers-say-theyre-productive-working-office/ Accessed 2020 <pgs.86-87>

The National Center for Fathering (NCF). The Extent of Fatherlessness, https://fathers.com/statistics-and-research/the-extent-of-fatherlessness/ Accessed 2020 <pgs.93-101>

Gaille, Brandon. 21 Compelling Motherless Children Statistics, https://brandongaille.com/19-compelling-motherless-children-statistics/ Accessed 2020 <pg.102>

The Trustees of Indiana University. Couples report gender differences in relationship, sexual satisfaction over time, https://newsinfo.iu.edu/news/page/normal/18996.html Accessed 2020 <pg.102>

Pew Research Center. Social Media Fact Sheet, https://www.pewresearch.org/internet/fact-sheet/social-media/ Accessed 2020 <pg.103>

Smith M.A., Melinda and Segal Ph.D., Jeanne. Well-Being & Happiness, https://www.helpguide.org/articles/mental-health/cultivating-happiness.htm Accessed 2020 <pgs.102-124>

Krznaric, Roman. Six Habits of Highly Empathic People, https://greatergood.berkeley.edu/article/item/six_habits_of_highly_empathic_people1 Accessed 2020 <pgs.107-115>

The Conversation. The dark side of supportive relationships, https://neurosciencenews.com/dark-relationship-support-15422/ Accessed 2020 <pgs.112-115>

Williams, Dr. Scott. Self-Awareness and Personal Development, http://www.wright.edu/~scott.williams/LeaderLetter/selfawareness.htm Access 2020 <pgs.113-143>

Divorce Statistics. How Much Divorce Cost In The USA, https://www.divorcestatistics.info/how-much-does-divorce-cost-in-the-usa.html Accessed 2021 <pg.121>

Toni Shiloh. How to Be a Princess: 7 Characteristics of a Princess. Retrieved June 12, 2022 https://arynthelibraryan.com/how-to-be-a-princess/

Simply Sinnara. Characteristics of A Princess. Retrieved June 12, 2022 http://www.simplysinnara.com/2018/04/characteristics-of-princess.html

Alive and Active Life. 12 Qualities Of Noble Character. Retrieved March, 2022 https://www.aliveandactivelife.org/articles/12-qualities-noble-character/

Colleen Florendo. If you have these 10 traits, you're a noble person with true integrity. Retrieved March 09, 2022 https://hackspirit.com/traits-of-noble-person/

Niccolo Machiavelli. The Qualities of a Prince. Retrieved March 09, 2022 https://phdessay.com/the-qualities-of-a-prince-by-niccolo-machiavelli/ "

Pediatric Academic Societies. (2000) Importance of Fathers in Children's Lives

https://www.newswise.com/articles/importance-of-fathers-in-childrens-lives

The Center for Parenting Education. PART I – THE BIG PICTURE:

TEACHING RESPONSIBILITY TO YOUR CHILDREN. https://centerforparentingeducation.org/library-of-articles/responsibility-and-chores/developing-responsibility-in-your-children/

The Trustees of Indiana University. Couples report gender differences in relationship, sexual satisfaction over time, https://newsinfo.iu.edu/news/page/normal/18996.html Accessed 2020 <pg.102